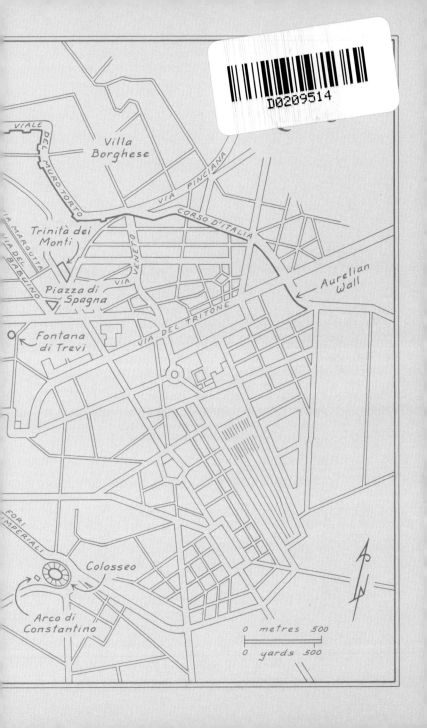

City of the Soul

Malibu

The Mouth of the Wolf

Horse Fever

The Killing Touch

The Dream Girls

Previews of Coming Attractions

The Americano

The Sweet Ride

Pirandello's One-Act Plays (translator)

*To Clothe the Naked and Two Other Plays by
    Luigi Pirandello* (translator)

The Self-Starting Wheel

Best Seller

The Fugitive Romans

PLAYS

The Executioner

Witnesses

Dialogue for a Dead Playwright

Ave Caesar

City of the Soul

A WALK IN ROME

William Murray

CROWN JOURNEYS

CROWN PUBLISHERS · NEW YORK

Published by Crown Journeys, an imprint of Crown Publishers, New York. Member of the Crown Publishing Group, a division of Random House, Inc. www.randomhouse.com

CROWN JOURNEYS and the Crown Journeys colophon are trademarks of Random House, Inc.

Printed in the United States of America

Design by Lauren Dong

Title page photograph © Merten / Getty Images / FPG

Map by Jackie Aher

Library of Congress Cataloging-in-Publication Data
Murray, William, 1926–
     City of the soul : a walk in Rome / by William Murray.
     1. Rome (Italy)—Description and travel.   2. Murray, William,
1926—Journeys—Italy—Rome.   I. Title.
   DG806.2 .M87   2003
   914.5′6320492—dc21   2002067428

ISBN 0-609-60614-X

10   9   8   7   6   5   4   3   2   1

First Edition

For Alice, Natalia, Julia, and Bill,
honorary Romans

"O Rome! my country! city of the soul!"

—Lord Byron

City of the Soul

One

THE ENTRANCE INTO the heart of Rome from the north is through a monumental medieval gate in the ancient Aurelian Wall that suddenly thrusts the visitor into the spacious magnificence of the Piazza del Popolo, one of the city's most beautiful squares. For about a year I walked under this portico every morning on my way to whatever the day would bring. The year was 1949 and I lived then in a small two-room apartment on the Via Flaminia, a couple of blocks away. It was the period of my life when I was studying singing, still hoping for a career in opera as a lyric tenor, while supporting myself as a part-time journalist, mainly as a stringer for the Rome bureau of Time-Life. I always tried to arrive in the piazza early enough to have a cappuccino at the Café Rosati, on the southwestern side of the square, from where I could sit out in the open, read a morning newspaper, and occasionally look out over the great sweep of space, punctuated at its center by the Egyptian obelisk of Ramses III, to the heights of the Pincio gardens across the way. Rome is nothing if not a feast for the eyes. I lived in the city then as an adopted Roman and thought that I would never leave it.

I had spent most of the first eight years of my life in Rome. My mother, Natalia Danesi Murray, was a native Roman, the oldest of three daughters born to an editor and printer named Giulio Danesi and his wife, Ester Danesi Traversari. Giulio died suddenly of septicemia in 1915, leaving Ester nearly penniless. The young widow went to work as a journalist to support herself and her children, became the first Italian female war correspondent by visiting the Austrian front in 1918, and went on to found and edit two leading women's magazines, until forced to flee to the United States in 1936 by her opposition to the Fascist government of Benito Mussolini. My mother had married an American talent agent, after whom I was named, but had soon after separated from him. She was in Italy with me when he went broke in the stock-market crash of 1929 and she went to work in the theater as an actress and singer to support us. When she brought me back to America in the fall of 1934, I spoke only Italian and French. I soon learned English, however, and became a totally American kid, refusing even to speak Italian at home with my mother and grandmother. My love of music brought me back to Italy in 1947, after the Second World War, when I was twenty-one. I could study there far more cheaply than in the States, and most of the great opera singers I admired were Italian. Within a year of my arrival I had again become fluent in the language and comfortably at home among the ancient stones of the city's *centro storico,* its historic heart.

I had also discovered that I had a family connection to the Piazza del Popolo. The square was named after the Church of Santa Maria del Popolo, first erected as a small chapel in 1099, diagonally across from where I sat every morning nursing my cappuccino. The site was chosen to liberate the populace from the frightening nocturnal apparitions of the hated Emperor Nero's ghost, whose tomb was reportedly located directly under where the main altar now stands. At the time the chapel was built, the piazza didn't exist; it was merely an open space of vineyards and vegetable plots. In 1227, Pope Gregory IX built the original church. It was torn down and replaced by the present one in 1472, under the supervision of Pope Sixtus V, who was also mostly responsible for the shape the piazza eventually assumed. He placed the obelisk, originally imported from Heliopolis by the Emperor Augustus, in its heart, providing a focus around which, over the centuries, the square assumed its present form.

There are now three churches on the piazza; in

1660 Pope Alexander VII commissioned the building of the twin edifices of Santa Maria di Monte Santo and Santa Maria dei Miracoli, at the southern end, from which three main avenues lead into the *centro*. But neither is as historically interesting or artistically significant as Santa Maria del Popolo, where, soon after my return to Rome, I was able to look up one of my ancestors, whom my grandmother had once described as an unprincipled thief.

The unprepossessing building nestles up against the Aurelian Wall, to the right of the Porta del Popolo and directly beneath the Pincio. It is a treasure trove of masterpieces, containing works by Raphael, Bramante, Sansovino, and others. Outstanding are the Pinturicchio frescoes in the main chapel behind the altar, and two famously magnificent huge paintings by Caravaggio, *The Conversion of St. Paul* and *The Crucifixion of St. Peter,* in one of the side chapels. When I first walked into this church, however, shortly after my arrival in Rome, I went initially in search of my ancestor, the unprincipled cleric from Ravenna who, according to family legend, had despoiled us of our patrimony by leaving everything at his death to the Church. I found his bust mounted high up with several others in a long, narrow side corridor to the right. Cardinal Carlo Traversario, with his long beard, tall miter, and strong nose, stared coldly back at me out of his sightless, bulging eyes as if to rebuke me for my effrontery. "He stole from the poor and gave to the rich," I remember my grandmother telling me, but then, like many Romans, she was a *mangiaprete,* a so-called priest-eater, someone who believed that too many of the world's injustices were due to the meddling in temporal affairs by members of the clergy.

FOR ALL OF my early years back in Rome, the Piazza del Popolo remains a constant, the scene of so many major and minor events. Its vastness and its curiously irregular shape contributed to its fascination. In the middle of the nineteenth century the Romans used to play at "blind cat," a form of blindman's buff in which contestants were blindfolded, whirled about a couple of times, and asked to reach the exits from the square into Via del Corso from the base of the obelisk. Few succeeded, a testimony to the deceptively irregular layout imposed on the square by a succession of architects and town planners, including Giuseppe Valadier, who later became famous for his designs in Paris.

Martin Luther is supposed to have fallen to his knees here when he first arrived in Rome, and held up his hands to heaven in thanks, though it did him little good later. The Romans themselves used the square as a promenade, for an evening drive, for carnival and other celebrations. During my time it became the site for the enormous and potentially violent rallies staged by Italy's Communist Party, then the second largest in Europe. From there, after a series of inflammatory speeches, the crowds would sometimes fan out to march through the city, under defiant revolutionary banners and shouting angry slogans. Occasionally the government's tough, truncheon-wielding security cops would break the meetings up, sending protesters fleeing into doorways and up side streets. I covered several of these events for *Time,* and once even found myself dragooned into participating in one by a Roman stonemason who had done some work for me and became a friend. He dragged me from the sidelines into the heart of the crowd to cheer and shout with everyone else.

Most of the time, however, the great piazza basked in the silence of history. There were very few cars then, and by nightfall none at all. Not only in the mornings but often in the evenings, after dinner, I'd meet friends back at the Café Rosati and we'd sit outdoors, chat, tell stories, and stare contentedly at the scene before us. When the automobile became dominant and pervasive in the early 1950s, overwhelming Italy's ancient towns under a sludge of vehicles, the Piazza del Popolo became a parking lot, while a honking flow of cars, motor scooters, and tourist buses inched past the café, spewing poison fumes toward its luckless outdoor patrons. The square today, however, has again been emptied of traffic and mostly returned to pedestrians, so that it's once more possible to enjoy it. "I was still afraid I might be dreaming," Goethe wrote in 1786, as he entered the city for the first time. "It was not till I had passed through the Porta del Popolo that I was certain it was true, that I really was in Rome."

Two

THE ONLY WAY to really enjoy Rome and to begin to understand the city is to walk about in it. It's not even necessary to follow any particular itinerary. I've always felt sorry for the masses of tourists who are yanked about from one great popular historical site to another in air-conditioned buses, or herded through museums and churches in unwieldy groups led by guides spouting endless statistics and nuggets of often unreliable information. What can they get out of such visits but a bewilderingly kaleidoscopic view of the capital's many wonders, a passing impression of historical time as reflected by such familiar monuments as the Colosseum or the Trevi Fountain?

No one should come to Rome for only a day or two; better to stay home and watch the Travel Channel. This is a city that makes demands upon your attention, that requires a commitment to leisurely exploration.

Its ancient ruins, its gleaming Renaissance palaces, its great Baroque basilicas and dozens of treasure-filled churches, its squares and fountains and statues, its maze of narrow cobbled streets, the very stones themselves, which exude an aura of time endlessly indulged, can only be appreciated in the intimacy of personal exploration. And even then you will find that whatever time you may have spent in the city, you will long for more. Like Hawthorne, Goethe, Byron, Keats, Shelley, Twain, and so many other artists and writers and just plain visitors, you will find yourself lured back to it time after time by the fascination it exerts. "For Rome one lifetime is not enough" is the apt title of one Roman author's cheerful reminiscences.

It is necessary, of course, to familiarize yourself with the basic layout of the *centro storico,* as well as the vast expanse of ancient Roman ruins now open to the public. I suggest the striking of a happy balance. When I brought my wife, Alice, to Rome for her initial visit in the spring of 1975, she spent her first five mornings in the city taking the guided tours that whisked her expeditiously to Rome's most celebrated monuments—the Colosseum, the Imperial Forum, the Campidoglio, the Pantheon, St. Peter's and the Sistine Chapel, the Castel Sant'Angelo, the Catacombs, the Trevi Fountain, the Circus Maximus, the Baths of Caracalla, the major churches and museums and the grander piazzas. In the afternoons, however, she struck out on her own, a reliable guidebook and map in hand, to immerse herself in the intimate life of the city's heart.

A walk anywhere in Rome cannot be hurried. I still like to stroll at random through the snarled cobweb of the *centro,* pausing every few yards to look around, then unfailingly up the building walls where, no matter how familiar the area or how many times I've already walked that way, I always spot something I haven't noticed before—a cornice, an inscription, a fragment of a ruin, an arch, a statue. Rome cherishes her past and nothing is ever discarded here, which is one reason why it took an entire generation to build a subway system. Everywhere the engineers dug, they came across some memento of the city's glorious past and all work stopped, often for months, while archaeologists and experts from the Department of Antiquities and Fine Arts evaluated the find and determined how best to preserve it.

The rules, whether enforced or not, never seem to go out of date. Recently on the Via Montoro, a narrow little street near the Campo dei Fiori, I glanced upward and spotted a marble tablet on the corner of a large seventeenth-century palazzo that read, "By order of the resident Monsignor of the streets, it is forbidden to discard rubbish in this place under penalty of fifteen scudi and other penalties in conformity with the edict promulgated May 22, 1761." I had never been in the

Via Montoro before or noticed such a sign, but since then I've become aware that it's to be found on the corners of many buildings all over the *centro*.

The scudo, a gold or silver coin issued all over Italy from the sixteenth century to the early nineteenth, is now a collector's item, but I suspect that somewhere, in some hidden nook of one of Rome's ancient government buildings, the Monsignor of the streets still sits at a desk emanating edicts. In Rome, no bureaucratic entity is ever allowed to die, a fact pointed out some years ago by the well-known journalist Luigi Barzini Jr. Somewhere, he maintained, in some Kafkaesque warren hidden from the prying eyes of inquisitive reporters, someone still administers an office overseeing the veterans' affairs of Garibaldi's Redshirts or the welfare of the Vestal Virgins. A walk in Rome is also an insight into the mysteries of survival.

OF THE THREE main arteries leading out of the Piazza del Popolo into the *centro,* the one I favor the least is the Via del Corso, which cuts straight through the heart of the city all the way to Piazza Venezia, with its medieval palace, now a museum, from whose balcony Benito Mussolini used to harangue the Fascist mobs, and the enormous gleaming white bulk of the Vittorio Emanuele Monument, completed in 1911 to commemorate the unification of the country and which now also houses the Tomb of the Unknown Soldier. Some people refer to the monument as a wedding cake, but to me it looks like an old-fashioned typewriter and I've always hoped in vain that someday it would be torn down. Its removal would provide visitors with direct access to the Campidoglio on its hilltop, with the Imperial Forum laid out diagonally in splendor behind it all the way to the Colosseum. A selfish pipe dream, because to many Italians the monument is as honored a relic as the Statue of Liberty or Paris's Arc de Triomphe.

The Corso has always been considered the city's main thoroughfare, even when it was merely a long, narrow street hemmed in on both sides by palaces, houses, shops, and the open stalls of street vendors. In the Middle Ages the Romans began racing horses down it from the obelisk to Palazzo Venezia, a practice that continued for centuries. Successive generations of popes periodically widened the avenue and banned the humbler merchants from the area. By the late eighteenth century it had become a daily rendezvous for the nobility and the upper middle classes in their horse-drawn carriages, which also attracted to the area the sort of elegant shops that catered to the wealthy. Mussolini, with his grandiose dream of recreating the Roman Empire, disfigured one whole section of the Corso by tearing down centuries-old houses in order to widen it still further, presumably for triumphal processions. One section now consists of several examples of the sort of imperial architecture the dictator fancied: great, gray, soulless monoliths embodying the Fascist dream of conformity and order at all costs. What Mussolini couldn't control or alter was the chaotic vehicular and pedestrian traffic that swarmed up and down the Corso all day long; it was neither dignified nor respectful. Exasperated, he decreed that people should walk in one direction only, on alternate sides of the street. That effort also failed, which may account for the possibly apocryphal story that the dictator, when asked by a foreign diplomat whether it was difficult to govern the Italians, replied, "No, it is not difficult, but it is useless."

Today's Romans are not the severe, self-sacrificing, humorlessly patriotic citizens of the Republic during the two centuries before the birth of Christ, nor are they the superbly arrogant conquerors of the world who flourished under the Caesars. What they are—cheerful, energetic, cynical, self-absorbed, shrewd, suspicious, profoundly human—can best be observed daily in the capital's streets and piazzas, especially along the Corso on weekends, when the avenue is closed to traffic, and festive crowds of pedestrians of all ages and backgrounds swarm past and into and out of its shops and cafés. No longer imperial, no longer elegant, the Via del Corso has been largely transformed into a shopping mall, with many of the typical franchises that now disfigure the historic neighborhoods of most great cities. And yet, even today, some remnants of the avenue's celebrated past remain, mostly in the form of commemorative tablets. In October 1786, Goethe settled in among a resident colony of German artists and intellectuals living in rented rooms at number 18, and Percy Bysshe Shelley began writing his poetic tragedy *The Cenci* in the Palazzo Verospi, now a bank directly across the way from the Rinascente department store.

A FAR MORE interesting outlet from the Piazza del Popolo is the Via di Ripetta, which ran down to the banks of the Tiber, where, in 1704, Pope Clement XI used stones stripped from the Colosseum to build a small harbor to receive goods being shipped downstream from Sabina and Umbria. The harbor has long since disappeared, after the construction of an ugly bridge across the river. I used this bridge every day for several months during a brief period of my life when I lived in an artist's studio on a rooftop from where I could look out over a portion of the *centro*. The setting was romantic, but the studio leaked water in torrents whenever it rained, and the toilet was an outhouse to which I had to sprint if I needed to relieve myself. I lasted about three months, until a January freeze forced me to move.

During that time, however, on my way up to the Piazza del Popolo I often passed between two of Rome's most fascinating monuments, the Tomb of Augustus and the Ara Pacis. The former was built by the emperor to contain himself and his relatives, that merry band which included his wife, Livia, who is suspected of having poisoned him, jolly old Tiberius, and assorted nephews, nieces, in-laws, stepsons, step-grandsons, and finally even the Emperor Nerva, who died in A.D. 98, eighty-four years after Augustus's demise. When Mussolini, who reportedly had plans to have himself entombed in it, ordered its restoration in 1936, the surrounding neighborhood was leveled and entire streets disappeared, leaving the monument exposed and isolated like, according to the Romans, "a rotting tooth." Today the huge mausoleum, surrounded by cypresses, is an awe-inspiring sight but not an attractive one, and it seems to be rarely visited. Perhaps this is because it has been encased in glass, as if to absent itself from any contact with humanity. It had been the site of a bullring, a garden, a concert stadium, and various other public venues. Now it basks in ominous silence, another testimony to the indifference of history.

The Ara Pacis, on the other hand, is a marvel of restoration. It is an altar of white marble surrounded by friezes depicting floral decorations and fauna and, on a side wall, a procession of dignitaries, including Augustus himself, other members of his family, and his retinue. Austerely simple, it was built in 13 B.C. to commemorate the emperor's military triumphs abroad. Unlike the tomb, the Ara Pacis is profoundly human and actually thrilling to contemplate, as if the figures in relief might turn and speak to us. The restoration of this extraordinary piece dates back to the late nineteenth century, when archaeologists began to study a number of fragments that had surfaced several centuries earlier and had been preserved in various private and public collections, including the Louvre in Paris. The re-creation of the Ara Pacis, finally completed in 1938, is one of the great achievements of archaeology.

During those early days of mine in Rome after the war, I paid little attention to these remnants of the city's proud past. I was too excited by my new life as a full-time voice student and participant in the postwar evolution of Rome, from the capital of a disgraced totalitarian state into a hub of democracy, to care about the past. I lived among these great mementos of history without actually seeing them or enjoying them, taking them totally for granted. I had been in Rome for over a year before I took the time to visit the Ara Pacis and the Tomb of Augustus, and then only because my Aunt Lea, who lived in a penthouse apartment on the Corso very near the sites, shamed me into it. She was scandalized by my ignorance. "You cannot live in Rome like a barbarian," she said to me. I didn't tell her that I hadn't yet bothered to go look at St. Peter's and the Sistine Chapel. She might have given up on me altogether.

Three

*I*N ROME THE statues speak. Some of them simply
because they are so magnificently lifelike that they
look as if they are about to say something; others
because the people of Rome over the centuries have
used them to give voice to their opinions. One of the
most famous of these talking statues is the one the
Romans dubbed "the baboon," which now occupies a
space up against the wall of a Greek Orthodox church
about halfway between the Piazza del Popolo and the
Piazza di Spagna, on the street named Via del Babuino,
the "Street of the Baboon." The statue is actually a rep-
resentation of Silenus, the drunken satyr who gam-
boled through mythology in company with his protégé
Dionysus, the god of wine and fertility. Here, in ruined
state, he is depicted lying in a tub and holding a small
bagpipe. The statue once adorned a fountain built by
Pope Gregory XIII in 1576, but it was temporarily

removed to the Via Flaminia in 1877, when the street was being widened and sewers built, then returned to its present location.

Most Romans have never bothered to learn who the baboon really was. A cardinal who lived in the neighborhood in 1590 mistook the satyr for Saint Jerome and used to kneel and tip his hat to it every time he passed. The people, however, saw in the bearded, reclining figure a reflection of their own cynical outlook regarding the exercise of power during the years when the city was ruled by a succession of mostly corrupt papal governments. They voiced their protestations of injustices by scrawling slogans, slurs, satirical verses, and defamatory remarks on the walls behind and around the statue. Occasionally they would deface the statue itself, as if they held it personally responsible for the wrongs committed.

The tradition continues. Despite every effort made by the municipal governments to clean up and defend the sculpture from these popular depredations, the Romans still use the baboon to voice their feelings, often these days against Americans. It's nothing personal; the talking statues always speak out against entrenched power, sometimes wittily, often brutally and viciously. Because the Via del Babuino is the most direct route between the Piazza del Popolo and the Piazza di Spagna, the square traditionally most frequented by foreigners, I still pass frequently by the baboon and always pause to find out what's on its mind. During the terrorist agitations of the 1970s, the so-called Years of Lead, the baboon regularly denounced the government and predicted its violent overthrow. Today, after a generation of prosperity and relative calm in the streets, the baboon rarely becomes incensed about anything except the fortunes of the capital's two professional soccer teams, though in the spring of 1999, during the period when the United States was dropping bombs on Serbia, I came across one disquieting exhortation: "U.S.A. assassins, we hate you!" There's nothing like a war to stir up public resentment and prod the statues into speaking out again.

I spent a lot of time in the late 1940s going up and down the Via del Babuino, with its many shops, still there today, that sell antiques and art objects. This was a period in my life when many of my friends were artists who lived and worked in studios on the Via Margutta, the shorter street paralleling the Via del Babuino. Every Saturday night for years the Bulgarian sculptor Amerigo Tot held an open house in his apartment on the Margutta where everyone was welcome and where, sipping wine and munching on cheese and salami, we'd argue and joke the night away. Tot, a gentle, civilized man with a forbidding appearance who sculpted enormous, heavy-breasted statues of naked women, enjoyed late in life a brief movie career when he appeared in *The Godfather, Part II,* in the silent role of a hit man. I hadn't seen him in many years and he looked much the same.

The Via Margutta is still a pleasant street to stroll along, with its many small art galleries and curiosity shops. It began to take shape around the middle of the sixteenth century and from the beginning became a center of art and culture, with an active Circolo Artistico, an artists' association that promoted the work of its members and threw lavish carnival celebrations that attracted artists, intellectuals, and potential patrons and buyers from all over the country. As time is measured in Rome, the Via Margutta can lay no claim to ancient glories, but I still enjoy it for its cheery, unpretentious atmosphere. "Can it be called a main street, this old Via Margutta," the Roman dialect poet Augusto Jandolo wrote of it in 1887, "which is prettier than uglier, even though there's nothing special about it? It's a quiet street, anything but solemn, made to work and to make love in." It probably derives its very name from a humble antecedent, the presence in the neighborhood in the 1580s of a popular barber named Giovanni Margutti.

LIKE MOST AMERICANS either living in the city or passing through it, I've always spent a lot of time in the Piazza di Spagna. For one thing, the American

Express office is located there, and I used to convert my dollars into lire at a small exchange office on the Via Propaganda Fide, just off the square. This office was run by pale monks from some Vatican order who offered a better rate than even the black market. I remember them vanishing with my dollars into the dim recesses of their quarters inside the vast bulk of their gloomy palazzo, before shuffling back toward me and unsmilingly thrusting wads of ten-thousand-lire notes at me. The building housed a religious institution founded by Pope Gregory XV in 1622 to instruct the young and propagate the faith throughout the world—evidently a profitable enterprise, to judge by the generosity of my money-changing monks.

The area was first called Piazza di Francia, after the church built on the hill overlooking it by the French monarchy in 1494, but took its present name from the embassy to the Vatican that the Spanish constructed in the early seventeenth century. Until then the area had been largely neglected, but by the end of the century it had become the hub for all foreign visitors to Rome. An early Italian guidebook described it as "much frequented by foreigners, also in summer by citizens, who flock to it toward evening to enjoy the cool air," and also the hotels, shops, cafés, and restaurants that flourished there. The list of famous names who have graced the piazza with their presence—from Stendhal, Goethe, and Balzac to Liszt, Wagner,

Rubens, and many more—is nearly endless. Every Englishman of note passed through or lingered awhile, to such an extent that the Romans began to refer to it as "the English ghetto." The poet John Keats died there of consumption on February 23, 1821, in a small house at the foot of the Spanish Steps facing the piazza. He was twenty-six years old. The house is now a museum containing the poet's death mask (showing him smiling peacefully), a collection of his works, and a library that includes the works of his contemporaries, most notably Byron and Shelley, and many relics of the period.

The presence around the piazza of so many wealthy tourists inevitably attracted some unsavory elements—thieves, pickpockets, con artists, and women of the sort the Romans sometimes referred to as "gallant little ladies." The last became a problem because for years there wasn't much the papal governments could do about them. Embassies enjoyed diplomatic immunity not only on their premises but in the surrounding area; Spain's diplomatic dominion extended to the adjacent streets as well as the square, and the working girls took advantage of it to move into the neighborhood. By August 1801, three years after this law was revoked, Pope Pius VII had received enough complaints to compel him to order a general roundup, not only of the gallant little ladies but of known criminals. One hundred and two women were condemned to five years in prison and thirty-three men to thirty lashes each. The grander courtesans, alerted in time by their protectors, fled. From then on they were forbidden to drive about the city in fancy carriages and, curiously, to bathe in the Tiber, which apparently had become another popular way of displaying their charms.

One of Rome's least attractive monuments is a massive column originally dug up elsewhere in 1778, then pretty much forgotten until Pope Pius IX decided in 1857 to erect it in the piazza to commemorate his promulgation three years earlier of the dogma of the Immaculate Conception. The statue of the Virgin, sculpted for the occasion and mounted on top of the column, was considered so ugly by the German historian Ferdinand Gregorovius that he described it as a champagne cork mounted upside down. Pasquino, the most eloquent and coruscatingly witty of the city's talking statues, chose to report an exchange between himself and Michelangelo's famous sculpture of Moses. "Speak!" Pasquino demands, much as the artist himself reportedly cried on completing the work. "I can't! My mouth is too small!" the Moses replies. "Then whistle!" Pasquino continues. "Yes, I'll whistle at the sculpture of the Virgin!" Moses responds. (In Italy, a loud whistle is the equivalent of a Bronx cheer, and a chorus of them is the same as a good round of booing.)

The outstanding feature of the Piazza di Spagna is the Spanish Steps, the great stairway leading up to the heights of Trinità dei Monti, with its French church and small obelisk, a Roman imitation of an Egyptian model. Approved under the reign of Pope Innocent XIII (1721–1724), the steps, 137 in all, were divided by three broad landings and designed by their creator, Francesco de Sanctis, so they would be appreciated from as far away as the Corso. In fact, one of the best views in Rome is to be enjoyed by walking away from the steps along the Via Condotti, then turning back to look at them. Around Easter, when it is banked in flowers, the stairway is particularly alluring, but it never fails to move me at any time of the year. It has always been a rendezvous for visitors and, beginning in the nineteenth century, a place where artists' models gathered, hoping to be employed by the painters and sculptors on their way to and from their studios on the Via Margutta. I used to hang out there a lot because, sooner or later, I could always count on bumping into someone I knew. There was a period when the stairs became almost impassable because they were suddenly taken over by street vendors peddling their cheap wares on cloths laid out on the stones, but eventually they were forced to move, and it's now once more possible to sit there in peace and enjoy the spectacle of the streets. On weekends, all of Rome seems to be passing through Piazza di Spagna.

At the very foot of the steps is one of my favorite Roman fountains, the Barcaccia, or "old boat." Built in 1623 by one of the famous Berninis, probably Pietro, the father of Gian Lorenzo, it was designed to recall the flooding of the piazza in 1621, when the Tiber spectacularly overflowed its banks all the way to the base of the Pincio, leaving in its wake the wreck of an old boat. The event provided Bernini with the inspiration he needed, and also helped him find a practical way to cope with the low pressure of the water in this part of the city, still supplied by one of Rome's most ancient aqueducts. The water spouting from the Barcaccia used to be the sweetest in Rome, but now drinking water from any public fountain anywhere has become a bit risky.

Four

THE LONG CLIMB up the 137 steps from the Piazza di Spagna, then right onto the Via Sistina, then left up the Via Francesco Crispi to the Ludovico quarter was an ascent I made often when I first came to live in Rome after the war. This was because my mother lived in an apartment on the Via Piemonte, four blocks beyond the Via Veneto, with its luxury hotels and fashionable sidewalk cafés. It was a largely residential neighborhood that had begun to attract wealthy visitors and residents after the creation of the Via Veneto in 1870. I liked the area as a sometimes welcome change from the crowding and confusion of the *centro,* even though it had none of the latter's charm. In 1952 I took over my mother's flat after her return to New York, and twenty years later I lived for another year one block off the Via Veneto in a tiny place on the Via di Porta Pinciana, directly across from the Aurelian Wall. I grew to love the wall as a symbol of Roman power and also because people lived in it, in small artists' studios carved out of its towers and thick bastions. It was named after its builder, Lucius Domitius Aurelianus, a warlike emperor elected to the supreme power by his soldiers in A.D. 270 and then slaughtered by them five years later. One of the recurring delights of Rome is that every section of the city, even in the newer quarters, has its own historical landmarks and stories to tell.

Just beyond the confines of the Aurelian Wall is the vast public park of the Villa Borghese, with its groves of umbrella pines, its open meadows and flower gardens, still reflecting in its general layout the landscaping taste of Cardinal Scipione Borghese (1605–1621), who wanted to re-create the effect achieved fourteen centuries earlier by the Emperor Hadrian at his estate in Tivoli. In scale alone the cardinal succeeded, while also building himself a villa designed in the classical style, not to be lived in but to show off his personal art collection, mostly of ancient Greek and Roman statues. Since then the villa as a museum had a history of ups and downs, even after it was bought by the nation in 1902. When I first wandered into it, it was gloomy and badly lit, with too many paintings crowded together on the walls. No one was ever quite sure what was to be displayed in it or how, and for three decades it was closed to the public for restorations, until finally it reopened in 1999 with a splendid exhibition of the sculpture of Gian Lorenzo Bernini, whom Cardinal Borghese knew well. Included in the collection are his *David* and *Apollo and Daphne.* Thirty years to restore a building is not very long, the way time is measured in Rome, and it was well worth the wait. The Borghese now happens to be one of my favorite museums, not only because of the beauty of the building itself, but because it's compact enough to be enjoyed in a single day, no minor virtue in a city that is itself a museum and where only a small fraction of what the past has yielded up can be put on display.

As a child I used to romp through the Villa Borghese, sometimes to watch the horse shows put on in the public riding rings or to visit the zoo, but my favorite trip was always down the slope of the great park to the terraced gardens of the Pincio, overlooking the Piazza del Popolo. Here there was always a Punch and Judy show that apparently had been there for hundreds of years, with its loudly sarcastic puppets violently belaboring one another while we children screamed in delight. It was a place for nannies and mothers pushing prams and for respectable ladies to have tea on the open terrace of the Casino Valadier. Later, I found out, it also served as a convenient rendezvous for lovers, who liked to stroll among the busts of celebrated citizens and heroes of the Risorgimento, sculpted and placed there at the urgings of the fiery Republican patriot Giuseppe Mazzini, Italy's Tom Paine. Unfortunately the Romans, with their cynical outlook on politics in general and their deep distrust of all public figures, soon got into the habit of knocking off the noses of the more than two hundred heroes on view, with the result that the city government has had to keep an expert restorer of noses on the public payroll.

THE CAFÉS LINING both sides of the Via Veneto between the huge bulk of the American Embassy and Consulate and the Aurelian Wall have always been heavily patronized by well-to-do Italians as well as the tourists staying in the fancy hotels, such as the Excelsior and the Flora. One of the great pleasures of Rome is being able to sit outdoors at the café tables to watch the world pass by. Along the Via Veneto, that world consists partly of the rich, the reckless, the naughty, and the beautiful. The street really came into its own beginning in the early 1950s, when Italy began to enjoy what the media called *il benessere,* or well-being, the term that defined the postwar economic boom that created a whole new middle class of citizens who for the first time in their lives could afford an automobile, a refrigerator, a summer villa by the sea, and other appurtenances of prosperity.

This headlong rush to the good life left in its wake a large segment of the population, the underprivileged and poorly educated citizens mostly living in the outlying slums of the large cities or left behind in their hilltop villages and abandoned countrysides. Nobody then, however, worried very much about them; the country had wholeheartedly embraced the values of an American-style capitalism, and the winners in the game hadn't the inclination or the time to pay much attention to the fate of the losers. Along the Via Veneto, especially after dusk, the winners celebrated, putting on a great, glamorous parade of entrenched wealth, instant celebrity, and desirable flesh that gripped the imagination not only of the Romans who participated in it but of people everywhere. Nothing caught that mood and time better than the director Federico Fellini's great movie *La Dolce Vita,* whose real protagonist was the freelance photographer Paparazzo, a name that has passed into the language to define a type, the unscrupulous invader of privacy and hustler of dreams with a flash camera in his hands. Today, two generations later, the Via Veneto has reverted to a less frenzied atmosphere, but still attracts to its outdoor gatherings more than a smattering of the rich and temporarily famous. Rome, as always, accepts them all as part of a passing scene. "In this country," the actress Anna Magnani, herself a quintessential Roman, once said, "only the monuments survive."

In Rome, not only the monuments, but all the relics of the city's past as well. At the foot of the Via Veneto sits the Capuchin Church of Santa Maria della Consezione, which has become a tourist mecca because of its underground chapel. The succession of six small rooms is crowded with the bones of more than four thousand monks who have been buried here. Subsequently dug up and put on display, the bones have been arranged into decorative patterns— arches of thigh bones, pyramids of skulls, frescoes of vertebrae, individual skeletons attired in their hooded robes and mounted in niches to grin at visitors. "Picturesque horrors" is how Mark Twain described the scene, while expressing admiration for the way the monks themselves had structured the exhibit, designs he deemed worthy of Michelangelo.

Even the Marquis de Sade was impressed. "I've seen nothing that has made such a vivid impression on me," he wrote, while going on to observe that the cemetery ought to be seen at its best, at night, by lamplight. He also noted that the living monks seemed to be a merry crew. "In Rome, they tell many stories about them which demonstrate that the present pleasures of life cause them to forget the dismaying image of the imminent destruction that awaits them."

One of these monks, Brother Pacifico, was so adept at forecasting the future that he attracted to the church great crowds of the faithful, who came not to attend Mass but to pick up a tip on the lottery. Pope Gregory XVI (1831–1846) was forced to intervene and banish the good friar from Rome. He was ushered as far as the Porta del Popolo by a mob of punters to whom he made a famous speech that included one last tip on the next drawing. Brother Pacifico was a Via Veneto kind of monk.

Five

*T*HE HANDFUL OF streets that lead out of Piazza di Spagna toward the oldest quarters of the city were the ones I frequented the most during my post-war years in Rome, and I still find myself strolling on one or two of them daily every time I come back. This is because each of them has attractions for the visitor and offers enticements few can resist, especially shoppers. Like most Roman streets, they are all named after some celebrity who happened to live there, an occupation, or a landmark. The Via Frattina recalls one of the first houses built in the seventeenth century in what was then still open country by the bishop of Amelia, Bartolomeo Ferratino; Via Borgognona was settled originally by a colony of Burgundians; Via della Croce, where Rubens and a group of Flemish painters once lived, recalls a giant cross mounted at the end of the street toward Piazza di Spagna; Via delle Carrozze because it was where people went to buy or lease horse-drawn carriages and where the vehicles were built, repaired, and cleaned; the Bocca di Leone, a cross street, either after the statue of a lion's head with an open mouth said to have been located there or because there was an opening that looked like a lion's mouth leading into a main sewer line; and the Via Condotti because under it flowed the water from the aqueduct that supplied the lower part of the city as far as the Tiber. That aqueduct, bringing water from the Alban Hills, south of the city, was named the Aqua Vergine (Virgin Water) and was built by Agrippa, Augustus's son-in-law, in 19 B.C. Legend has it that the source of the stream was indicated to a group of thirsty Roman soldiers by a young local girl, hence the name. It was such a popular discovery that the Romans, the world's greatest partygoers, celebrated the event for fifty-nine days, sacrificing who knows how many animals and gladiators in the process.

Of the streets in this part of town, my wife's favorite is the Via Frattina, because of its many specialty shops, boutiques, and a couple of cafés with outdoor tables from which one can survey the passing squadrons of determined shoppers while resting one's feet. It also provides easy access to Via Bocca di Leone, with its famous Hotel Inghilterra, lone survivor of all the fancy establishments catering to foreigners that once flourished in the quarter. The hostelry is now a luxury inn with rooms priced at hundreds of dollars a night, but when I stayed there in 1947, during my first few days back in the city, I rented a small single room on an upper floor for six dollars a night. An open terrace connected all of the rooms on my floor, which was mostly occupied by single young people, and adventure beckoned. My wife and I love the Inghilterra, she because it has the cleanest, most modern ladies' room in the area, and I because its small, elegant little bar serves the driest, coldest martini in town.

Other streets in the area offer inducements, the Via della Croce its food shops and *trattorie,* the Via Borgognona several luxury stores and Nino's, long one of the city's best restaurants, specializing in Tuscan dishes. But for sheer elegance and history the Via Condotti has always been the place to stroll, to buy, to linger in envy and admiration, and just for the sheer pleasure of watching the Japanese hordes battle their way into Gucci. The Condotti is a street not to seek a bargain in, but to admire the toys and the trappings the wealthy accumulate for themselves. And then, at the point when you're ready to drop from the sheer excitement and fatigue the spectacle induces, there is the Caffè Greco, the ultimate refuge from life's daily struggles and obligations.

At the bar of the Greco, customers are engaged in an active pursuit of coffee, drinks, and hors d'oeuvres to be imbibed standing up, while cell phones ring and calls are dialed, a frenetic scene that reflects during shopping hours the activity of the street outside. But inside, in the quiet procession of dimly lit rooms furnished with small, marble-topped tables, banquettes, antiques, walls displaying paintings, etchings, lithographs, and framed mementos, the Greco remains what it has always been, a refuge for conversationalists, artists, thinkers, and now, inevitably, exhausted shoppers and tourists.

The Caffè Greco was named after Nicola di Maddalena, the Levantine Greek who founded it in 1760 at a time when the area was full of hotels and *pensioni*. From the first day it became the favorite gathering place for the city's colony of eminent visitors, then a haven as well for local artists and writers. Tennyson and Thackeray used to pop in from the rooms they were staying in across the street. Stendhal, Gounod, Wagner, Byron, Liszt, Keats, and Shelley were habitués. The great Italian poet Giacomo Leopardi used to drop in, as did the sculptor Antonio Canova and the playwright Carlo Goldoni, who reportedly wrote several of his 150 plays on the premises. In the 1780s, when Goethe was in town, the rooms became the headquarters for the often noisily rambunctious German artists' colony. Gogol wrote much of *Dead Souls* in here. And from its creation the Greco was an obligatory oasis for the aristocratic English on their grand tours of the Continent.

The historical popularity of the Greco with its distinguished clientele has undoubtedly protected it from being demolished or modernized. To judge by early illustrations and photographs, it looks pretty much the same as it did in its first heyday two centuries ago. The aging waiters in their black tails look as if they've just stepped out of a movie set. What is different is that few artists or writers now spend much time in it, probably because it has become a little too popular and too full of tourists. Nevertheless, here and there, at some corner table or other an artist or writer can occasionally be spotted, either sketching or scribbling, seated advertisements for the locale's past. Among the illuminati, of course, is a sprinkling of poseurs and the obsessed, none more typical than the splendidly bearded Sicilian professor Illuminato Dispenza, who spent twenty years of his life at the same corner table trying to solve the mathematical problem of squaring the circle. "On the sudden," wrote Shakespeare, "a Roman thought hath struck him."

Six

*R*OME HAS NEVER been considered a musical city, in the sense of Milan, with its great opera house, La Scala, or Naples, with its centuries-old tradition of popular song. The city's Teatro dell'Opera has only rarely in its history achieved a standard of performance comparable to that of half a dozen other Italian opera houses, mainly because its management has always been influenced by shifting political forces at city hall. And then, too, the Romans themselves have never been either great opera fans or willing even to pay full price for a ticket, in a city in which many households include a relative or two employed in some ministerial office with access to free passes. The deficits have been enormous, and inevitably have to be made up out of public funds, a situation that tends to inhibit innovation and artistic excellence. I never minded. As a voice student in Rome during the early postwar years,

I went as often as I could to the opera house, standing at the back of the orchestra with other young singers and debating with them in the intervals the merits, or lack thereof, of this or that diva. It was a heady time, and for me the city was full of music.

I had grown up with the sounds of Rome in my ears. My mother, who had an untrained but beautiful dark voice and accompanied herself on a guitar, taught me a number of *stornelli,* the Roman street songs, largely improvised, that sounded faintly Arabic, full of melodic twists and turns in hauntingly plaintive minor keys. Then there were the popular songs, not as famous as those of Naples, but well known all over the country, especially when sung by such pop artists as Renato Rascel, Gabriella Ferri, Giorgio Innovato, and others largely forgotten now but celebrities in their own time.

For me as a music student, Rome was a festival of song. Every weekday I walked down the Via Condotti or the Corso and turned into Via Fontanella Borghese, where on the fifth floor of an ancient palazzo I attended the vocal academy run by the Count and Countess Calcagni, an elderly couple who taught or tried to teach several dozen of us how to sing. The hour-long lessons cost the equivalent of fifty cents each, and one could also sit in on everybody else's lessons and participate in duets, trios, *concertati.* I ate, breathed, and lived opera, and I don't think I've ever been happier in my life.

This part of Rome, surprisingly enough, has a rich theatrical and musical history. The enormous Palazzo Borghese itself, which dominates this medieval quarter, was nicknamed "the harpsichord" by the Romans because it was shaped like one. Finished in 1609, it was bought by Cardinal Camillo Borghese before he was elected Pope Paul V. The Borgheses were the richest family in Rome, perhaps in all of Italy, and the palace still belongs to them, even though a financial crash in 1887 wiped them out and forced them to sell almost everything, including their priceless library. Cardinal Scipione Borghese put together his art treasures there before transferring them to his villa in the park.

Over the past two centuries the palazzo has accommodated a number of wealthy and influential characters, none more eccentric than Pauline Bonaparte, the emperor's favorite sister, who married Camillo Borghese in 1803. Then only twenty-three years old and very beautiful, she lived in a fourth-floor apartment above the main entrance, where she entertained a series of lovers, reportedly used her ladies-in-waiting as footstools, and had herself carried to her bath by a large black attendant. Today the palazzo houses the Circolo della Caccia (the Hunt Club), the most exclusive private club in Italy, as well as private apartments and offices. Unfortunately, it's not open to the public except for one or two special days a year, but through its open portal can be glimpsed the vast gardens, the many statues, and the colonnade of ninety-six Ionic and Doric columns, ranged in pairs, that support the upper stories.

In the piazza just beyond the palace is a large open-air market where for years I bought old opera scores, records, and prints, mainly from an old Roman named Morosi, whose family has had a pushcart in the square for generations. Every time I came back to the city over the years I would stop by to say hello and to make an occasional small purchase of a print, an old book, a fragment of a manuscript, a medal, an ancient coin. As he aged, Morosi seemed to blend into his merchandise, sinking back into the inner recesses of his pushcart, sitting quietly inside it on cold days, bundled up against the weather in a heavy overcoat, scarf, and hat. He's gone now, but his son Paolo has taken over, having added a second pushcart to the original one and training his own children to take over from him.

The square was also the site of a popular supper club patronized by artists and musicians, including Francesco Paolo Tosti and the poet Gabriele D'Annunzio, who in 1895 rented rooms on the premises above the restaurant. He was then thirty-two years old and recalled the period as one of "splendid poverty . . . but with the joy of being able to breathe grandly." Tosti lived nearby on the Via Prefetti in what D'Annunzio recalled as a large gloomy apartment "full of dark hallways and hiding places." When the composer was in form, "he would make music for hours and hours without tiring, forgetting himself at the piano, occasionally improvising."

Carlo Goldoni lived in the neighborhood, in the square that would be named after him, between November 1758 and August 1759, during which time he wrote *Gl'Innamorati* (*The Lovers*). So did Pauline Bonaparte's lawyer, Giuseppe Vannotelli, who had twelve children, all but two of whom became musicians. They created a family musical salon that attracted Liszt, Bizet, and Gounod to their premises, where they put on concerts and staged performances of oratorios and operas. The music pouring forth from those rooms attracted passersby, who would linger under the windows to listen, just as in my own time the vocal outpourings from the Calcagnis' apartment not only never brought complaints from their neighbors, but only observations on the quality of the singers. I do remember one complaint, on a summer afternoon when, planted by an open window, I cracked a high note at the end of an aria. "Aah-ooh," I heard a voice call out from the courtyard below, "change your profession!"

Eventually I did.

Seven

*E*VERY YEAR NOW, when my wife and I return to Rome in the spring, we follow a daily routine. From our small hotel a few blocks away, we stroll to the Piazza Rotonda and settle at an outdoor café table facing the central fountain of the square and the great portico of the Pantheon, architecturally and aesthetically one of the most beautiful buildings in Rome. Nothing could be more pleasant or rewarding, even on a rainy day, than to sit out there in the comforting shade of an umbrella while sipping a caffè latte, munching on a croissant, and contemplating this astonishing relic of ancient Rome's grandeur. Not even the obnoxious presence in the piazza of a McDonald's can spoil the time spent there.

The walk from our hotel, a block or so from the Piazza Borghese, is in itself an education in the drama of daily life as it has been lived in this part of the city

for centuries. All of these little streets—the Via
Metastasio, Via della Stelletta, Via Pozzo di Cornac-
chie, Via Giustiniani, and others—look much as they
did in the Middle Ages, and are lived in by working
citizens plying some of the same trades as their ancestors. The whole quarter bustles with life, and every
building has a story to tell. We are now in the very
heart of the *centro,* where myth, fancy, rumor, and
tradition blend indistinguishably into history. In the
Church of the Maddalena, for instance, on the street
named after it that leads directly to the Pantheon, is
the tomb of Teresa Benicelli, who died at the age of
twenty-three in July 1843. She was beautiful, from a
newly rich and ennobled family who dreamed she
would marry worthily and well. Instead she fell in love
with a lowly dragoon of the papal regiments named
Pio Pratesi. The family arranged to have Pratesi transferred to Viterbo, after which the girl sank into a deep
depression. Her doctor informed the family that she
was beyond hope. In desperation, Pratesi was sum-
moned to her bedside, where he cradled her in his
arms, but all she could do was whisper, "It's too late."
Three days later she died. The whole city went into
mourning, and a tremendous crowd attended the
funeral. Pratesi went home and tried twice to shoot
himself, but each time the gun misfired. Inspired by
what he considered divine intervention, the twenty-
five-year-old cadet became a monk and, two years

later, as Father Pacifico, celebrated his first Mass over the tomb of his beloved Teresa. Shakespeare would have loved this story, which, if nothing else, proves that the Romans, for all their vaunted cynicism and indifference to history's misadventures and injustices, are as subject as anyone else to true romance.

Traditionally the Romans have never been sentimental about their great heritage, and it's a miracle that so much has survived from the past since the collapse of the empire fifteen hundred years ago. Buildings and streets have been constructed out of the marble and stones stripped from monuments; gold, brass, and silver have been appropriated to decorate the palaces and villas of popes and nobles; statues, paintings, and relics have been vandalized or carted off to be sold to private collectors. Then there have been the periodic foreign invasions that have contributed to these depredations. Only the sheer amount and size of what remains have prevented the city from becoming a wasteland, though I suspect that if the *centro* had been turned over to American engineers, nothing would have remained, and freeways and shopping malls would have replaced the forums, the temples, and the Colosseum.

The Pantheon is a typical case in point. It was supposedly built in 25 B.C. by the Roman consul Marcus Agrippa, as testified to by the Latin inscription over the portico, but actually it was the Emperor Hadrian who, between A.D. 120 and 125, was responsible for its present shape. Its outstanding feature is its dome, larger than that of St. Peter's and still considered a marvel of engineering. The central eye, at the apex of the dome, that illuminates the whole interior, is about twenty-seven feet in diameter. It would be hard to imagine a more perfect construction, or one more worthy of being preserved, but the building would probably not have survived if it hadn't been sanctified by Pope Boniface IV in 608 and converted into a church. (Legend recounts that a flock of demons was observed escaping upward through the eye of the dome during the dedication ceremony.) This didn't prevent the building from being looted of its sheets of bronze, first by Byzantine troops in 655 and later by Pope Urban VIII of Rome's Barberini family, an event immortalized by Pasquino, Rome's most famous talking statue, who quipped in Latin, "What the barbarians did not do, the Barberini did."

Over the centuries, the Romans have treated the Pantheon as an interesting relic, but not one to become excessively concerned about. Until 1847 the piazza was the site of an open-air fish market, and the portico was periodically used as an art gallery. Until a few years ago, the frontal view of the great building was often obscured by gigantic tourist buses that used to park directly in front of it and keep their engines running, poisoning the air with noxious fumes, and still today, sellers of trinkets and hustlers of all kinds ply their dubious trades under the columns by the entrance.

Inside, however, the building remains a serene and awesome triumph of the spirit, a testament to a divinity that embraces a larger human theme than doctrinaire Christianity. Its stoic calm is inspirational. When Rome was being sacked in 1779 by French troops, and their commanders were systematically looting the city, many of the soldiers and petty officers, as well as hundreds of Romans, gathered in the Pantheon to protest, and succeeded in bringing the matter to the attention of the Directory, which put a stop to it. It's appropriate, too, that Raphael is buried here, the artist who died in 1520 at the age of thirty-seven and whose epitaph commemorates a man who was so talented that even "nature feared to be outdone."

DIRECTLY BEYOND THE Pantheon and to the left of it is the Piazza della Minerva, with its charming church named Santa Maria over Minerva. It was erected over the ruins of a temple built by Pompey the Great and dedicated to Minerva, the goddess of wisdom. In the center of the square stands one of the city's most entertaining small monuments, the statue of an elephant supporting on its back an Egyptian obelisk, one of three found among the ruins in the

area. The epigraph at the base of the monument, dic-
tated by Pope Urban VIII, declares that the selection
of the elephant, "the strongest of the animals," was
designed to impart an impression of solid thinking in
a sound mind. Gian Lorenzo Bernini, who designed
the monument, apparently had no such intent in
mind. Invited to tour France by King Louis XIV in
1665, he found himself so famous that everywhere he
went he was besieged by ogling crowds of admirers.
Exasperated by so much attention, the artist was heard
to say, "What is this? Have I become some sort of rare
beast, an elephant?" Back in Rome, he designed his
monument to reflect his French travails, choosing the
statue sculpted by Ercole Ferrata as its dominant feature. The Romans, with their gift for irreverence and
irony, soon began referring to it as "Minerva's flea."

The unprepossessing little church, with its unique
exterior, was built in 1280 and contains a number of
extraordinary treasures, including the tombs of several
celebrated Roman families and monuments to various
important popes and cardinals. The body of Saint
Catherine of Siena, renowned for her mystical visions
and revelations, and influential in persuading Pope
Gregory XI to leave Avignon and return to Rome in
1377, is buried under the main altar. In the Carafa
Chapel are Fra Filippo Lippi's extraordinary frescoes,
including his *Assumption of the Virgin,* which occupies
an entire wall. Also in a corner of this chapel is the

tomb of Pope Paul IV, the fearsome pontiff who was responsible for enclosing the Jews in the ghetto and launching the Inquisition on the Roman populace. He was so unpopular that when he died in 1559, a Roman mob laid siege to the Dominican monastery next to the church and tried to burn it down. The Dominicans had carried out the pope's orders, which they apparently took permanently to heart, because it was there, four generations later, that Galileo was brought to trial for his heretical views concerning the planets revolving around the sun and was forced to abjure them. It is not for nothing that the Romans have acquired a reputation for disliking the clergy.

The church's most famous treasure is Michelangelo's statue *Christ Carrying the Cross,* sculpted between 1514 and 1521. So many worshipers bent to kiss the statue's foot that a sandal was added later in order to keep it from being worn away by so many fervent lips. The Romans may not like their popes, but they revere their artists. They also appreciate inspired advice. There used to be an inscription somewhere in the church that I was never able to locate but which read, "In order not to be killed by Rome's foul air, it is necessary to purge oneself every week, avoid bad smells, not tire oneself much, not suffer either hunger or cold, to renounce all faults, love, and to drink hot liquids."

Perhaps no other church in Rome is so revered by the citizens as this one. When Anna Magnani, Italy's most celebrated stage and movie actress, died on September 26, 1973, it seemed entirely appropriate that her funeral service be held here, in the heart of the old city she had come to symbolize and where she had passed most of her life. The enormous, grief-stricken crowd that came to say good-bye to her spilled out of the church and filled the square to overflowing. And when her coffin was raised up to be carried out, the people applauded, as if to thank her for what she had come to represent for them—the vital spirit of their city.

Eight

I ONCE BECAME INVOLVED in a heated discussion with a friend who lived in Paris concerning the relative merits of Paris and Rome. The French capital, he maintained, had, among its many other virtues, the most beautiful open spaces in the world— the Place Vendôme, the Place de la Concorde, the Tuileries, and half a dozen other justly celebrated spots. All I said to him was "Piazza Navona." He paused, stunned, then looked at me and smiled. "You win," he said. "God's waiting room."

The first time I ever set foot in it, I simply stood at one end of it for at least ten minutes and stared. I spent the next three hours sitting at a café table taking it all in—its great open sweep of elliptical space punctuated by its three glorious fountains and hemmed in by its churches, palaces, and ancient rust-colored houses, their terraces awash in flowers, overhead the deep, blue cloudless sky of a Roman spring morning. "This is not a piazza," wrote Belli, abandoning for once his cynical take on man's achievements, "it's a countryside, a theater, a fair, a delight."

Piazza Navona is not only the most exquisitely beautiful square in Rome, it's also the beating heart of the city. No other spot is so affectionately regarded by its citizens, who for nearly two thousand years have flocked to it for the pleasures it has provided. It was created by the Emperor Domitian (A.D. 81–96) as a sports stadium and was called the Circus Adonalis, later corrupted to n'Agona, then eventually to Navona. For centuries it survived as an arena for jousts and other forms of athletic contests, but also as a gathering place for celebrations and various festive occasions. No gladiatorial bouts, no killings, no executions, no tortures, no bloodletting took place here. Offering pleasurable pursuits, the great arena became a haven for people bent on enjoying themselves.

In 1477, Pope Sixtus IV made the piazza the site of the city's daily marketplace, and all traces of the ancient Roman arena were wiped out by the construction of inns, taverns, and restaurants. Then, in the mid-sixteenth century, Pope Innocent X decided to convert the space into a glorious testimonial to his own greatness. His family had come to Rome from Umbria in the middle of the fifteenth century, and lived in a modest house on the square that he ordered to be torn down and replaced by an enormous palazzo designed by Giordano Rainaldi. He wanted three great fountains, so he arranged to have the waters of the Aqua Vergine pumped into the square and commissioned Bernini to design the central one, the Fountain of the Four Rivers, surmounted by the obelisk that had been found lying in pieces along the Via Appia. In 1652 he hired Francesco Borromini, Bernini's hated rival, to help build the Church of Sant' Agnese in Agone over the spot where, in 304, Saint Agnes, then only thirteen years old, was publicly stripped and martyred. Borromini designed the Baroque façade of the church, whose walls incorporated remnants of the ancient Roman stadium.

In his efforts to glorify himself and his family, Pope Innocent succeeded in creating an architectural and aesthetic marvel that permanently enshrined the Piazza Navona in the hearts of the Roman populace. Undoubtedly its most beautiful single feature is Bernini's fountain, with its allegorical figures and symbols, but the whole of the space gives the impression of having been laid out by a single great artist. Luckily, nothing has been done since then to mar the effect the piazza achieves, a timeless rendering of the Roman spirit.

What Pope Innocent failed to do during his reign was endear himself to his people or even to his own family. He was mean, weak, and corrupt. As he lay dying in 1655, his relatives and servants grabbed everything they could lay their hands on, even the brass candlesticks burning beside his bed. His despised sister-in-law, Olimpia Maldachini, dragged his last two chests full of money from under his bed and made off with them, leaving the pope to die alone, lying under a single ragged blanket. No one wanted to pay for his burial, until at last a monsignor coughed up a few scudi to pay for having the body carted away at night to the Church of Sant' Agnese, where later it was entombed in an ugly monument no one visits.

As with every great Roman site, the piazza abounds in legends. The most common of these concerns the rivalry between Bernini and Borromini. The statue of the Plate River by Bernini seems to have an arm raised in protest toward the Church of Sant' Agnese, as if afraid the building might collapse on it, while the statue of the Nile turns its back on the church, as if horrified by its ugliness. The statue of Saint Agnes, however, answers with a gesture to assure the world that all is right and that nothing will happen. The animosity between the two artists was real, but the story is false. Bernini began his work in 1650, while Borromini's contribution to the church did not begin until 1653, three years later.

Every day the Piazza Navona attracts hordes of visitors, many of them tourists but also just ordinary citizens for whom the square has become a second living room. The space is lined by cafés, restaurants, wine bars, and small shops, while in the center, around and between the fountains, dozens of painters, sketch artists, trinket salesmen, mimes, and other popular entertainers hustle for a living. Permanently closed to traffic, Piazza Navona has become a pageant and a huge shopping mall, never more so than during the Christmas holidays, when the piazza disappears under a great tide of pushcarts and stands selling religious figures, entire *presepi,* toys, candies, all kinds of dainties. The climax comes on the night of Epiphany, January 6, when a good witch named Befana flies around all over the city delivering presents to worthy children. The adults celebrate the occasion by flocking to the square to make noise, blowing on whistles, horns, pipes, and every kind of loud instrument. On New Year's Eve it used to be the habit to throw unwanted pots, pans, and other household utensils out the window, but so many people were injured over the years that the practice is now discouraged. Noise, however, is never discouraged in this city, where silence arrives only in the late night hours and departs with the sunrise.

Of all the stories I love about life in Rome, one of my favorites has to do with the Roman guide who is showing off the city to an unimpressed American tourist. Everywhere they go, the American proclaims that at home his country boasts far more impressive sights than even the Colosseum or St. Peter's. Finally the Roman takes his charge through a back door into a small *trattoria* on a short street off the Piazza Navona. They have a glass of wine together, after which the guide ushers his charge out the front door into the piazza itself. "What's this?" the American inquires, gazing around. "This?" the Roman replies. "Oh, it's the courtyard of the restaurant."

JUST BEYOND THE Piazza Navona, at the corner of Palazzo Braschi, stands the mutilated statue of a Greek warrior, probably Menelaus, thought to be in the act of defending the body of Patroclus, slain by Hector during the Trojan War. The fragment was discovered in 1501 and was used at first every April 25 as a site for academic and literary types to attach their epigrams and observations, usually obsequious and flattering to the rulers in power. This soon changed, however, when the Romans began to make of the statue a focus for their discontent. They named it Pasquino, in memory of a local tailor who had lived in the area and had become famous for his acidic comments and wise-cracks about the authorities and their misuse of power. These observations were either attached to the base of the statue or scrawled on it, and the practice became so popular that people made it a point to flock to it every morning to read what had been written there before someone could take it down or erase it. The sayings became famous—in English, satirical writings posted in public places are known as pasquinades—and the fragment soon became the most celebrated of the city's talking statues. The hated Olimpia Maldachini, for example, was immortalized in four Latin words: *"Ulim pia, nunc impia,"* which can be translated as "Once pious Olimpia, now impious."

For centuries the talking statues in Rome represented the only opposition press, the single outlet the people had to vent their contempt of, or anger with, the papal governments. Unsurprisingly, these often savagely witty comments were not enthusiastically received at the Vatican, and attempts were made by several pontiffs to muzzle the statues, especially Pasquino. In 1522, Pope Hadrian VI wanted to have it thrown into the Tiber, but was dissuaded from doing so because he was warned that "the frogs would croak louder from the water." Terrible punishments, including the death penalty, confiscation of property, and public humiliation, were threatened for any printed libel "in the nature of a 'pasquinade.'" Pope Pius VIII posted guards around the clock. But nothing worked; the talking statues continued to speak out. At the height of Fascism's triumphs, when Adolf Hitler visited Rome to find the city adorned by triumphal arches made mostly out of cardboard, Pasquino commented,

"Rome of travertine / now dressed in cardboard / salutes the pale one / her future boss."

Nothing could permanently shut Pasquino up. I like to think that it's because of his outspoken presence that the small piazza in which he stands also became known for the number of bookstores in the immediate vicinity. Belli, whose usually tart observations masked a fanatical adherence to the status quo, wondered in one of his dialect rhymes why anybody would want to buy a book. "What can you learn from so many books?" he wrote. "Take a book on an empty stomach, and after you've had it for a few hours, tell me whether you're happy or have eaten too much. What did the mission priest preach? Books are not for Christians. My children, please don't read them."

Nine

OR MANY YEARS my Aunt Franca lived in
a large duplex apartment overlooking the
Campo dei Fiori, the noisiest piazza in Rome. Whenever I stayed with her during the 1960s and 1970s, I
occupied a bedroom that looked directly over the
square. I can't imagine now how I stood it. The racket
began in the very early morning hours, when the first
iron shutters of the neighborhood shops and canteens
would be rolled up and workers would begin to set up
their pushcarts and stands for the day's business. By
dawn the square had been transformed into a sea of
gray canvas umbrellas sheltering the merchandise on
sale, everything from edibles of all kinds to clothes,
shoes, kitchen utensils, luggage, toys, records, all sorts
of household items. Since 1869 the Campo dei Fiori
has been the site of the city's central outdoor marketplace, transferred there from the Piazza Navona, then
undergoing extensive repairs and renovations.

Even during the late-afternoon hours, after the departure of the shoppers, when the stands and push-carts and umbrellas had all been stashed away for the day, the clamor persisted. Kids played pickup soccer games, religious processions and bands would come marching through, political parties with their bull-horns held rallies, and honking car traffic and motor scooters swept past. The only respite would come sometime between two and three A.M., when for a couple of hours the piazza seemed to be holding its breath, readying itself for a new assault on the senses.

Partly because of the noise, and partly because of the petty crime in the area, my aunt eventually moved away to a modern flat off the Via Cassia, on the northern outskirts of the city. I began to stay in small hotels and rarely ventured into the Campo dei Fiori, especially during the last few years, after it became the nighttime rendezvous for the young, a huge outdoor singles scene catered to by a host of wine bars, small fast-food emporia, cafés, and disco joints blaring rock music through their open door-ways. There's no respite now in the Campo dei Fiori from noise at any time of the day or night. Many of the residents of the quarter, especially the rich, who bought apartments here when local real estate was cheap and it became fashionable again to live some-where in the *centro* rather than in the more modern sections of town, have defended themselves by investing in air-conditioning and noise-proof, double-paneled windows.

The Campo dei Fiori is not one of Rome's prettier scenes. The piazza seems hemmed in by the burnt-orange and amber-colored houses around it, and an air of doom seems to hang over it, even at noon on crowded market days. It has an unsavory history. It was here during the Inquisition that Jews and heretics were put to death. The nearby Via della Corda was named after a medieval torture. People caught cheating in the grain market were tied at the wrists and hoisted into the air. Heavy weights were attached to their ankles, stretching their bodies to the utmost, and they were then allowed to drop toward the ground just far enough to jerk their arms out of their sockets. This practice wasn't abolished until 1816.

Of all the victims who perished here, the most famous is Giordano Bruno, the Dominican monk who was burned alive on January 20, 1600, as "an impenitent, tenacious, and obstinate heretic." He lived up to his billing, having responded to the verdict against him by saying, "Perhaps you tremble more in pronouncing the sentence than I in receiving it," and refusing to kiss the crucifix offered to him on his way to the pyre. Bruno had dared to doubt the dogmas of the Trinity and the Incarnation, and had championed the astronomical theories of Copernicus. His problem was that he read too much and didn't know when to keep his mouth shut. An appropriately gloomy statue of him was erected in the center of the piazza on June 9, 1889, and carries the following inscription: "To Bruno / of the Century by Him Divined / Here / Where the Pyre Burned." His presence seems to hang over even the most festive goings-on in the Campo, where the only other decorative touch in the square is a small stone fountain in the shape of a soup tureen that by day's end is filled with refuse—peelings, lettuce leaves, rotten fruit—dumped there by passing vendors.

The piazza was named either after Flora, the Roman mistress of Pompey the Great, whose theater occupied the eastern end of the space, or because it had once been an open field, presumably full of flowers. It flourished in medieval times as the main square through which important visitors and religious processions passed on their way to and from the Vatican. Some of the oldest hotels in the city—del Leone, della Nave, della Luna, dell' Angelo, della Campana, several others—were built around it, while the adjacent streets took on the names of the trades practiced in them. One of these hotels, l'Albergo della Vacca (Hotel of the Cow), was owned by Vannozza Catanei, thrice married but best remembered as the faithful mistress of Rodrigo Borgia, who became Pope Alexander VI. She was the mother of Lucretia, Cesare, and two other children. She was also a terrific entrepreneur, managing her successful hotel and buying and selling shops, restaurants, and other properties in the vicinity. Somehow she also managed to be a wife to three different husbands, none of whom ever complained about her.

JUST BEYOND THE Campo, in a long, rectangular piazza named after it, stands the enormous and spectacularly elegant Palazzo della Cancelleria, once the Vatican chancery and considered by many to be the most beautiful Renaissance palace in Rome. Newly cleaned, like so many of Rome's grandest monuments, it gleams like a great jewel in its relatively humble setting, at the edge of the noisy and crowded Campo. It was built in 1486 and cost sixty thousand scudi won gambling by a nephew of Pope Sixtus IV, Raffaele Riario. Originally thought to have been designed by Bramante, who didn't come to Rome until 1499, it was more probably the work of Andrea Bregno, though Bramante may have designed the courtyard, its most spectacular feature, with forty-four granite columns adorning the porticoes. The stones used for its construction were stripped from the Colosseum and several Roman baths. No one is quite sure about the Cancelleria's exact origins because the city was sacked in 1527 and all the records regarding it were destroyed. We do know that the frescoes in the vast salon were painted by Giorgio

Vasari and two assistants in a mere hundred days. When Vasari boasted to Michelangelo about this accomplishment, the latter replied, "It looks it."

The great building incorporates within its walls the small Church of San Lorenzo in Damaso. When Napoleon invaded Italy, his troops stabled their horses in it, but in 1807 Cardinal Carafa had it restored and in 1818 it was finally reconsecrated. When my grandmother Ester Danesi Traversari died at eighty-eight in her small apartment, we attended a funeral Mass for her here. She had never been very tolerant of the Church and certainly was not a believer in many of its more dogmatic pronouncements and rituals. In the end it didn't matter. It seemed entirely appropriate to me that she should have been mourned and laid to rest in the city she had loved all her life. And I remember sitting there that morning in the small, austere church, surrounded by the majestic beauty of the chancery, feeling only an enormous sense of peace and fulfillment.

Even more beautiful in my eyes than the Cancelleria is the Palazzo Farnese, in the piazza named after it on the other side of the Campo. The square has been kept clear of youthful celebrants as well as traffic because since 1871 the palace has been the site of the French Embassy and is therefore guarded around the clock by carabinieri and police. Alessandro Farnese, who became Pope Paul III in 1534, spent a fortune on the building, which took so long to construct that to get it finished, Pasquino was forced to appeal for help to the people of Rome: "Alms for the building [of the Farnese]!"

Alessandro had plenty of money, but he was tight with it. He owed much of his fortune to his sister Giulia's good looks, which attracted the eye of the Borgia pope, Alexander VI. He made her his mistress, replacing Vannozza Catanei. Favors and money flowed toward the Farnese family, and Alessandro was able to finish building his palace. He hired Antonio Sangallo to design it, then, after the latter's death in 1546, called in Michelangelo to complete it. Both inside and out, the palace is somberly magnificent, with its serene façade designed by Sangallo and its upper story by Michelangelo. Because it is still the site of the French Embassy, the building can only be visited a few days a year and on some Sunday mornings. Among its many pleasures is the main gallery, whose ceiling depicts classical scenes from Ovid's *Metamorphoses,* painted by Annibale Carracci. The artist had expected to be well rewarded for his efforts, but received a payment of only five hundred gold scudi. Carracci gave up painting, fled to Naples, then came back to Rome, where he sank into depression and despair, became a drunk, and died at forty-nine.

For a couple of weeks during the summer of 1949, I visited the Palazzo Farnese every night. I had fallen in love with a young woman with whom I had struck up a conversation one morning outside the Colosseum. It was an innocent affair, but we saw each other every day, toured the city together, dined, kissed passionately in the shadows of the buildings as I walked her home. She was the daughter of a French nobleman and granddaughter of an English diplomat, and was staying as a guest in the sheltered confines of the great palazzo. She never introduced me to any members of her family, and always kissed me good night under the arch leading into the courtyard of the embassy. One day I called for her and found her gone. Every time I pass the Palazzo Farnese now, I find myself wondering what became of her.

Ten

I N THE EARLY spring of 1949 I was hired as a
stringer by the Rome bureau of Time-Life. I had
heard about the job from an acquaintance at the bar
of the Foreign Press Club, where I used to hang out
in the late afternoons. The bureau chief was a man
named George Jones, who saw in me talents I didn't
know I possessed. He immediately put me to work on
a possible story coming out of a section of Rome I
had never even heard of, the ancient ghetto along the
banks of the Tiber across from Trastevere. Because I
was the only person in the office who spoke Italian,
Jones must have thought me uniquely qualified to
interview the residents of the quarter, but I have no
idea what made him believe I could get a story out of
the assignment and get it down on paper. Whatever
the reasons, his blind faith in me abruptly launched
me on a different path, even though it was several

years before I abandoned any hope of a career in opera to become a full-time writer.

I had always known vaguely that Italy had a Jewish population, but had not become really aware of it until the late 1930s, when a number of my mother's old Roman friends showed up in New York as fugitives from the racial laws imposed on the country by the Fascist regime. Not even my mother had known that they were Jewish, because she had grown up in a society that didn't distinguish between races. Rome's Jews had been around practically since the beginning of the republic, and had once flourished as the city acquired its empire and its riches. By the time my mother was born, they had become integrated and accepted into the society.

The first recorded contact came in 161 B.C., when a Jewish leader named Judah the Maccabee asked for Rome's protection against the Seleucid dynasty in Asia Minor. By 69 B.C., when Pompey the Great conquered Palestine and made it part of Rome's province of Syria, there were several thousand Jews living in Rome, and their numbers grew with the arrival of slaves and prisoners, most of whom were eventually set free. With added immigration from the Levant and Egypt, the colony swelled until it consisted of between thirty and forty thousand people. When a revolt broke out in Palestine in A.D. 67, however, and took three years to crush, during which many thousands of people died and Jerusalem was sacked, the Romans became less tolerant of the Jews in their midst, and began to regard them with suspicion. The Arch of Titus, erected at the foot of the Palatine in A.D. 81, commemorates the Roman victory over the Jews and depicts the prisoners and booty brought back into the city by the Roman army led by the Emperor Vespasian's son Titus. And the first restrictive measures against the colony, in the form of a tax, the so-called *fisca judaicus,* were imposed by Vespasian.

After that the Jews pretty much dropped out of the city's recorded history, surfacing only from time to time as the victims of various restrictive measures imposed by the popes or outbreaks of prejudice. In 1007, for example, we hear of the murder of three rabbis, and in 1020 of an attack by a mob convinced that the Jews were to blame for an earthquake. It wasn't until 1555 that the colony reappeared in full form as the subject of a bull issued by Pope Paul IV condemning it to be confined to a small area along the bank of the Tiber across from Trastevere, where most of the Jews had been living. The Jews were to be shut off from their fellow citizens by a wall and forbidden to engage in all forms of commerce except the sale of old clothes and junk. They were also to wear the color yellow, caps for the men and shawls for the women. The ancient buildings were packed close together along narrow streets and alleys where the sun rarely penetrated and the whole quarter was frequently inundated by the dirty waters of the Tiber. It wasn't until 1870, after the unification of Italy, that the walls of the ghetto were finally demolished, as were most of the houses along the waterfront. The Tiber was tamed by the construction of an embankment and new buildings went up, including, in 1904, the main synagogue, with a gleaming aluminum dome that testifies eloquently to the enduring faith of its people.

When I arrived at the entrance to the old ghetto that morning in early spring, I was immediately struck by the picturesque beauty of the setting. It consisted of several blocks of houses lining an avenue called the Via Portico d'Ottavia, named after the portico originally built in 149 B.C., then rebuilt in 23 B.C. by the Emperor Augustus and dedicated to his sister Ottavia. The rectangular space, enclosed by three hundred columns, included temples to Jupiter and Juno, as well as libraries and public meeting places adjacent to the immense Theater of Marcellus, also completed by Augustus. All that survives is a corner of the original portico and the Theater of Marcellus itself, which was converted in the Middle Ages into a Renaissance palace housing the Orsini, one of the most powerful families in Rome. The street extended for several hundred yards to the Piazza Costaguti and the Via Arenula, a busy avenue now clogged with traffic. On one side of the Via Portico d'Ottavia were the synagogue and the unprepossessing buildings put up after the partial demolition of the quarter, but on the other were the ancient houses of the ghetto, jammed in close together and separated only by narrow alleys meandering away between the dark walls of still other *palazzi,* some of which, like those of the Mattei and the Cenci, had dark, romantic histories.

My job that first morning was to interview the residents of the quarter concerning the possible return to the area of a woman named Celeste Di Porto, who had lived there with her family. Originally nicknamed Stella (Star) for her beauty, she acquired a more sinister one, Black Panther, for her activities during the war. She had escaped the Nazi roundup of the Jews in the quarter on October 16, 1943, and had gone on to become the mistress of a Fascist officer. She had escaped deportation by fingering for the authorities some fifty of her fellow citizens, most of whom perished either in the concentration camps or during the massacre at the Ardeatine caves outside the city, where the Nazis executed 335 people, seventy-three of them Jews, because of a Partisan attack that had killed thirty-three of their soldiers. The Black Panther had reportedly been paid five thousand lire, about fifty dollars, for every person she turned in. Arrested by the Allies after the liberation of Italy, the Black Panther had been released from prison recently and was reportedly planning to return to the quarter, where she still had relatives. Some of the people I talked with that morning swore they would kill her if she dared to show up.

The Di Portos were one of the oldest Jewish families in Rome. They had supported themselves for centuries by selling clothes and household goods in the open-air market in Campo dei Fiori, where they had long operated a licensed stall. None of the surviving members of the family would talk to me that morning, but I was told that they had all disowned the Black Panther and that they would be happy to see her brought to justice if she dared to show up. What no one could understand was how she had managed to get herself released and could even consider coming back to the quarter. As it turned out, the Black Panther never did return, and no one knows what happened to her, but I had my story and it was published in the following week's edition of *Time,* my first successful venture into journalism.

THE OLD GHETTO is still a fascinating place to visit, with its surviving ancient houses and its weight of tragic history. The *palazzi* have fragments of marble columns and cornices embedded in their walls, and the alleys still wander off into sunless courtyards and between dark stone walls. Every foot of ground has its story to tell. At one corner of the street stands the Church of San Gregorio, with its inscription in both Latin and Hebrew over the entrance: "I have stretched out my hands every day to an unbelieving people," the opening sentence reads, "who have walked in a way that is not good, after their own thoughts." Near the Portico d'Ottavia itself is the Church of Sant'Angelo in Pescheria, which incorporates a portion of the ruin into its façade. Here, on occasional Sundays between 1572 and the 1800s, the police would round up whatever residents they could find to be subjected to conversionist sermons by Dominican priests. The spirit of Pope Paul IV, with his lean inquisitorial countenance, still haunts the area.

On a wall of a perfectly preserved little Renaissance house that is now the local headquarters of the Department of Antiquities and Fine Arts hangs a large white marble tablet, placed there on October 25, 1964, to commemorate the twentieth anniversary of the Partisan Resistance. It reads as follows:

> *On October 16, 1943,*
> *here began*
> *the merciless hunt of the Jews*
> *and two thousand ninety-one Roman citizens*
> *were dispatched to a ferocious death*
> *in the Nazi extermination camps*
> *where they were joined*

by another six thousand Italians,
victims of infamous
racial hatred.

The few who escaped the slaughter
the many local sympathizers
invoke from men
love and peace,
invoke from God
pardon and hope.

Of the 1,127 people taken away during that first roundup in the ghetto, including eight hundred women and children, most were sent in boxcars to Auschwitz. Only fourteen men and one woman survived to come home a year and a half later. A tour of the ghetto is not only a reminder of how appallingly the human race can behave, but also a testimony to the immortal spirit of a community. "And of this people, to which fate has entrusted the charters of mankind and which Christianity has, so to speak, displaced from its heritage," wrote the German historian Ferdinand Gregorovius in 1853, a century before these events, "there dwell here in the ghetto one of the oldest and historically most remarkable remnants, upon which history has exacted its great and tragic irony."

Eleven

A DECADE OR SO ago, when the Palatine and the Imperial Forum were temporarily closed to visitors because of the danger of cave-ins and falling stones, an American entrepreneur from California offered to buy the Colosseum. He offered a million dollars in cash, declaring he would spend another million to fix it up and would recoup his investment by charging admission to the restored monument. Rome's journalists had a field day with the story, which they used to belabor the municipal authorities for having in effect done nothing to preserve and restore the great tourist sites from the city's glorious past. They pointed out that the American had at least proposed doing something, whereas inertia was the order of the day at city hall.

No one who has not visited Rome can possibly imagine how difficult, if not impossible, it is to preserve and care for the estimated eighty million "important pieces" that constitute the city's patrimony. Not only do all the great buildings, ruins, fountains, catacombs, statues, and fragments on view have to be cared for, but also the many thousands of small objects—the humble remnants of an entire civilization—that are now stored away unseen in various storerooms. They surface only occasionally in the form of special exhibits mounted in some museum or other, but most of the time they have been consigned to permanent oblivion.

Luckily, under an enlightened new city administration, and with the new millennium and the Holy Year looming, much was done not only to preserve and to restore the great monuments, but also to clean up the churches and palaces sullied by decades of polluted air. They now literally gleam as they did when they were first built. Even the ordinary Roman citizens who complained most loudly about the inconvenience of having to live in what amounts to an open-air museum have voiced approval of what the municipal administration, under its dynamic young mayor, Francesco Rutelli, accomplished. A walk today into any piazza in Rome will confirm what has been done. The citizens are still able to go about their daily chores, setting up their outdoor booths in the shadows of great temples and churches, hanging their washing out to dry over the ruins or the terraces of ancient villas, playing soccer over the cobblestones between fountains, columns, and statues, integrating their immediate needs and concerns into these relics of the past. Life in Rome is a kaleidoscope of quickly changing scenes, a montage of past and present fusing into a single, often confusing whole.

Nothing, not even the Colosseum, so embodies the city's grandeur as the Campidoglio, the piazza designed by Michelangelo on the Capitol, the most famous of the city's seven hills. For most of the Middle Ages the square faced out toward the Imperial Forum and the Colosseum, but around 1536 Pope Paul III commissioned Michelangelo to restructure it so that it faced in the opposite direction and was framed by three great palaces—the Palazzo Nuovo, the Palazzo del Senatore, and the Palazzo dei Conservatori. The approach to it is up a gently inclined flight of steps built to welcome to the city the Holy Roman Emperor Charles V, who approached in a procession that passed under the Arch of Titus, crossed the Forum, then under the Arch of Septimius Severus, and so on, up the ramp where the pope and his cardinals awaited him. The gentle slope of the ascent is in sharp contrast to the earlier steep stairway next to it, built in 1348, up to the Church of the Aracoeli, to celebrate the end of a terrible plague. Michelangelo's design reflected a gentler, more humane age. To set it all off he chose to design the podium on which he placed the bronze equestrian statue of Marcus Aurelius, mounted on his great horse, his hand outstretched in benediction or welcome. It is the only surviving example of the great bronzes the Romans built and, like the others, it would almost certainly have been melted down if it hadn't mistakenly been taken for a statue of Constantine the Great, the first Christian emperor. It had been standing in the piazza in front of the Church of San Giovanni in Laterano, from where Michelangelo rescued it.

Many Romans are indifferent to the fate of their great monuments and simply take for granted that they will always be there. Not so with the statue of Marcus Aurelius, which is generally beloved. About ten years ago, when it was found to be suffering from the ravages of time and the city's polluted air, it was carted away for restoration to the Instituto Centrale del Restauro. It took several years to repair it, during which a fierce debate broke out in the press about what to do with the statue. The experts wanted to protect it from the elements and put it on permanent display in one of the Capitoline palaces, while the public seemed to favor returning it to its post on Michelangelo's podium. An ancient proverb proclaims that Rome will survive as long as the Colosseum stands, but most Romans believe that is equally true of the statue of Marcus Aurelius. In the end a compromise was reached. A copy of the horseman was made and now occupies Michelangelo's podium, while the original has been put on display under glass inside the Palazzo Nuovo.

The Palazzo del Senatore is still the seat of city government, but the two flanking palaces now make up the Capitoline Museum, which houses the greatest collection of statuary in the world. It cannot be seen and fully appreciated in a single visit, but, like the Louvre, has to be nibbled at a few rooms at a time. Among the famous treasures on view are the *Boy with the Thorn,* the colossal head of Constantius II, the *Capitoline Venus,* and the *Marble Faun,* as well as the series of busts of ancient Roman celebrities and ordinary citizens who provide a tremendous panorama of the sort of people who built and maintained for centuries an empire that dominated Western civilization. The emperors and their women are impressive enough, but the busts of unknown Romans, such as that of the anonymous middle-aged man looking back at us from the third century after Christ, testify to a race of conquerors and administrators whose like has never been seen since. The early Roman faces recall the republican virtues of the first settlers—humorless, resolute, determined—while the later ones reflect the virtues and vicissitudes of entrenched power. Consider, for instance, the humane beauty in old age of Augustus, as compared to the ferocious cruelty of Caracalla and his vicious successor, Heliogabalus. The whole history of the empire can be read in the expressions of these remarkable busts.

Of all the sculptures on display my personal favorite

is the *Capitoline She-Wolf* in the Palazzo dei Conservatori. The piece was probably sculpted by the Etruscan artist Volca of Veri, sometime between the end of the sixth century and the beginning of the fifth century B.C. No one knows how it happened to survive through the city's turbulent history, but somehow it did, perhaps because no other work so directly and eloquently testified to the city's birth. In 1509 the Florentine sculptor Antonio Pollaiuolo added the twins Romulus and Remus suckling at the wolf's swollen teats, thus ensuring that the statue would become the symbol for the whole city, to an even greater extent than the immortal cipher SPQR, which today appears all over town, even on sewer lids. It stands for the Latin words *Senatus Populusque Romanus,* "the Senate and People of Rome." Someone early on, perhaps Pasquino or one of the other talking statues, chose to translate the phrase differently as *Sono porci questi Romani,* or "They are pigs, these Romans." Having ruled over most of the Western world for a thousand years, the Romans know how to be irreverent about themselves.

Last year, when I went once again to see the marvels on display in the museum, I discovered that one could go up to the roof, where the administration has opened an outdoor café and restaurant. It provides the most magnificent view over the whole city, with its towering ruins, great church cupolas, and open rooftop terraces awash in greenery, small trees, and flowers.

The newly refurbished palaces shine like great jewels in this setting, while overhead flocks of swallows sweep about in search of insects and periodically the air resounds to the clamor of church bells calling the faithful to prayer and tolling the hours. I was transfixed by the scene, the whole mighty weight of history displayed as if for me alone—a sight no one should miss on any visit to this city, whether the first or one of many. "History is the witness that testifies to the passing of time," wrote Marcus Tullius Cicero in the first century B.C. "It illuminates reality, vitalizes memory, provides guidance in daily life, and brings us tidings of antiquity."

Twelve

I N 1962 my first wife and I lived with our two small children in a section of Rome known as the Aventino, after another of the fabled seven hills. Whenever we invited guests to visit us, I used to delight in giving them instructions on how to get to our apartment. "From Piazza Venezia," I would tell them, "take the Via dei Fori Imperiali toward the Colosseum, turn right at the Arch of Titus and proceed, keeping the Circus Maximus to your right and the Baths of Caracalla to your left, until you reach the Piazza Albania. If you get to the Pyramid of Cestius and the Aurelian Wall, you've gone too far. Turn back and you'll find our apartment house on your right, facing the Aventine."

The great fact of life in Rome is residence among the ruins. Even if you live in one of the newer fashionable residential sections, such as the Parioli, or in the outskirts of the city, the chances are that somewhere in your neighborhood some memento of the past—the fragment of an ancient aqueduct, a ruined watchtower, a Roman tomb—will become a daily feature of your life. The municipal government does its best to oversee and defend these remnants of past glories from the depredations of time and lootings by passersby, but it's often a losing battle. The Department of Antiquities and Fine Arts employs only a couple of dozen archaeological inspectors, whose job it is to patrol their assigned sections of the city, make reports to the authorities, and recommend courses of action. They are all overworked and underpaid, and their task would seem to be a hopeless one. Most of them, however, are fiercely dedicated men and women who somehow manage, against overwhelming odds, to defend and protect the city's amazing artifacts.

In addition to the roving inspectors, the city employs hundreds of guards to oversee the treasures in the museums and the forums. There never seem to be enough of them. At one time or another these great sights are closed to visitors, sometimes for renovations, but often only because there aren't enough people available to staff the sites. The Romans, who are accustomed to living among the ruins, are often exasperated by having to cope with the inconveniences arising out of the demands imposed by the hordes of tourists swarming through the most popular sights.

They often complain that Rome is, after all, not just an open-air museum, but a world capital and the seat of the nation's governing bodies. Some attention ought to be paid to the citizens' needs, not just those of the tourists. When the city government a few years ago proposed closing the Via dei Fori Imperiali permanently to traffic, there was a great cry of protest from the citizens living in the vicinity, who would then be compelled to get to their jobs and run their household errands by having to thread their way daily through the narrow, already congested streets behind the forums. A compromise was reached calling for the banning of traffic only on Sundays and certain other selected days of the year, including most national holidays. It satisfied no one, but then Rome is a city populated by cynics and protesters.

During the years I lived in Rome, I rarely, after my first weeks in the city, decided to devote a whole day to visiting an archaeological site or a great museum. I lived in the city the way most Romans did, incorporating into my daily life the existence of these ruins and monuments as part of an organic whole. My personal needs and desires were reflected in the choices I made. I spent hours, for example, in the great, tumbled remnants of the Roman Forum because I had fallen in love. In fact, I had met the woman I'll call Maggie on the terrace of the Capitoline Hill overlooking the Forum from behind the Palazzo del Senatore. She was

blond, young, slender, with cool blue eyes and a gen-
erous mouth, and she was leaning against the railing of
the terrace while staring down over the vast panorama
of Rome's past, a blue guidebook in her hand. I don't
remember exactly what I said to her, but she agreed to
let me show her around. I had been living in Rome
for about two years by then, and fancied myself an
expert.

Maggie knew much more than I did; she had stud-
ied her guidebook and knew exactly what we were
looking at as we strolled in the heat of the summer
afternoon sun through the whole expanse of the
Forum all the way to the Colosseum. It was one of the
great experiences of my life, because the very stones,
if you know what you are looking at, seem to speak,
to articulate their own histories. Maggie pointed out
the Comitium, a small open space where, from various rostrums, orators addressed the people during the
years of the republic. Over there was the Basilica Giulia, dedicated by Julius Caesar in 54 B.C., one of several built in the Forum. The basilicas were large open
spaces under vast ceilings and divided by one or two
rows of columns. They were used as gathering places,
for law courts, for business affairs, or simply as refuges
from the heat of the midday sun. Their architectural
styles, copied from the Greek, were incorporated into
the manner that shaped the churches built in the Middle
Ages. The Curia, the large red-brick building to the

right of the Comitium, was the house of the Senate, where for over a thousand years the people's representatives continued to meet even long after their legislative powers had been stripped away by the emperors. In A.D. 357, the golden statue of the Goddess of Victory that stood on an altar at one end was removed by imperial edict, then returned to her post until 394, when she vanished forever, a victim of the rise of Christianity and the banishment of the pagan gods. In the seventh century the Curia was converted into a church and so survived intact into the present. On the other side of the Comitium is the Lapis Niger, a black marble slab containing the oldest Latin inscription known anywhere and considered by some to be the actual tomb of Romulus, though that has been hotly debated by scholars for centuries.

The most dramatic ruin in this whole area is the Arch of Septimius Severus, erected in A.D. 203 by the emperor in his own honor. It was such an impressive monument to the city's great history that when it was decided to honor the arrival of the Holy Roman Emperor Charles V by having him and his retinue pass under it, two churches and several hundred adjoining houses had to be torn down to make that possible. From that time on, the newly crowned popes would follow a similar route when they proceeded on foot from St. Peter's to the Lateran to confirm their assumption of temporal power. The Pontifex Maximus was considered the heir to the throne of the emperors, even though his domain was purportedly limited to the spiritual, a fact that Pasquino and the other talking statues never allowed him to forget.

One of the oldest traditions of ancient Rome concerns a great hole in the middle of the Forum, which, according to legend, was bottomless and could never be closed until the city's most precious object was hurled into it. A Roman warrior named Marcus, dressed in full armor and mounted on his horse, thereupon leaped into the chasm, which immediately closed over him. All that remains is the scar left by his sacrificial gesture.

My favorite temple in Rome is the small circular one staffed by the Vestal Virgins, whose job it was to tend the sacred fire on the altar of the goddess. The Vestals were enlisted at the age of ten for a period of thirty years and lived in a house next to the temple. The survival of the city was supposed to depend on the fire never being allowed to go out, and on the virginity of the women who tended it. If the fire failed, they were whipped; if they lost their virginity, they were buried alive. Also in the temple was the Palladium, a statue of Pallas Athena purportedly brought to Rome from Troy by Aeneas. The Vestals were greatly loved by the Romans, who allowed the order to survive until A.D. 394, long after Christianity had become the dominant state religion, and then it took an imperial decree by the Emperor Theodosius to put an end to the sect.

The three Corinthian columns that stand in isolated splendor beside the temple of the Vestals are what survive of the Temple of Castor and Pollux, one of the oldest sites in the Forum, dating back to 484 B.C. and built to celebrate an early victory of the Romans at Lake Regillus, a few miles north of the city, over the Tarquin dynasty. Castor and Pollux, the twin brothers of Helen of Troy, had apparently intervened to ensure the victory and then, mounted on their white horses, had brought news of it back to Rome.

The little Church of Santa Maria Antiqua is the oldest site of Christian worship in the city. It was consecrated as a church sometime in the fifth century and restored in the seventh century by Pope John VII. It contains some remarkable frescoes depicting a crucifixion and other religious scenes, probably painted by Byzantine artists whose work greatly influenced the way Roman churches were subsequently decorated.

Touring Rome's outdoor archaeological sites can be an exhausting pastime, as I pointed out several times to Maggie that first afternoon. She laughed and pressed on, guidebook in hand, pulling me along in her wake. She had recently moved to Rome from South Africa, and told me that she lived with her husband, a scriptwriter, in a penthouse apartment overlooking the Piazza di Spagna. Since my interest in her clearly went beyond friendship, I expected she would thank me for my company and speed me on my way at day's end. I was wrong. We became lovers that evening, before she returned home, and for two weeks we met every day to go sightseeing and make love afterwards in my small apartment on the Via Flaminia. Her husband was too busy working on a screenplay to pay any attention to her, so perhaps this was her way of avenging herself for his disinterest in her. I'll never know. All I do know is that one day, after another long tramp in and out of various catacombs and churches, she abruptly ended our affair by shaking my hand, giving me a last quick peck on the cheek, and telling me not to call her again or make any attempt to see her. I was heartbroken. It was two months before I saw her again, this time with her husband and a group of their friends at the bar of the Foreign Press Club. She introduced me around as a casual acquaintance she had encountered one day in the Forum. "Bill is an expert on Rome," she said. "I learned more about the city's history from him than you can imagine." She threw back her head and laughed, and I remember thinking I'd found no better way to tour an ancient site than by making love among the ruins.

Thirteen

*T*HE TWO MOST popular monuments in Rome
are the Colosseum and the Castel Sant'Angelo,
both of which have long, bloody histories behind them.
The Colosseum, the older of the two, has become the
symbol of Rome, its great yawning façade staring out
at us from book covers, paintings, prints, lithographs,
and postcards to testify to the city's imperial past. It was
originally called the Flavian Amphitheater, after the
three emperors of that dynasty who built it. It was
begun by Vespasian, carried on by his son Titus, and
completed under the reign of Domitian in A.D. 80. At
its dedication by Titus, several thousand animals were
slaughtered and the games, featuring three thousand
gladiators, lasted a hundred days. It eventually became
known as the Colosseum either because of its colossal
proportions or after the erection nearby of a huge
statue of the Emperor Nero, later destroyed.

The shape of the great building, which could accommodate a hundred thousand spectators, was probably inspired by the design of the Theater of Marcellus. The outer wall was constructed of enormous blocks of travertine clamped together by iron bolts, and was four stories tall, the three lower ones composed of arches interspersed by columns. The wall is 157 feet high, with projecting so-called *consoles* that supported an awning to provide shade. The arena itself also consisted of blocks of travertine over which sand or sawdust was strewn during the games, and it was surrounded by a fifteen-foot wall, the *podium,* to protect the spectators from the animals and participants. The best seats, closest to the arena, were occupied by the emperor and his retinue, the nobles, and the Vestal Virgins, as well as the *editor,* the supervisor and impresario of the games. The humbler spectators sat in the upper rows, while the beasts and participants, including, in later years, unarmed Christians, awaited their turns in the arena in holding areas below ground level.

It's hard to account for the bloodthirstiness of the ancient Romans, those otherwise severe arbitrators of a legal system on which ours is modeled, and who ruled over an empire whose survival depended on the impartial administration of justice. There's no trace of that, or any sort of moderation, in the history of the Colosseum, where the numbers of animals and gladi-

ators slaughtered yearly seem monstrous. The gladiatorial contests are believed to have originated in the
ancient Etruscan custom of slaying captives and slaves
in public shows, and were first reported in Rome as
early as 264 B.C., when 120 gladiators fought for three
days to commemorate the deaths of two Roman
noblemen. Gladiators also fought at private banquets,
and the practice became so popular that more than ten
thousand of them battled to celebrate the victory of
the Emperor Trajan over the Dacians. By the time
Spartacus organized his revolt, he was able to raise
from the gladiatorial ranks an army of sixty thousand
men, most of whom died with him at the hands of
the Roman legions sent to crush the rebellion.

The Christian Emperor Constantine was the first
ruler to attempt to outlaw the games, but he got
nowhere; they were too popular and continued to
flourish for another seventy years. In 404, during one
of these gladiatorial contests, an Eastern monk named
Telemachus rushed into the arena to attempt to stop
the fighting, but was cut down by order of the Praetor
Alybius, who was annoyed at the interruption. The
monk's sacrifice, however, earned him sainthood and
succeeded in ending the gladiatorial games when the
Emperor Honorius banned them. Fights between and
with wild animals continued for another eighty years
until an edict of Justinian in 526 finally put an end
to them.

From then on, the Colosseum, abandoned to the ravages of time, wind, fire, and weather, slowly began to fall apart. Invading barbarians periodically looted it, making off with its metals and ornaments. Still, the great building survived and attracted to it every visitor, hostile or friendly, to the city. It was a visiting Anglo-Saxon monk who, early in the eighth century, first propounded the theory that the Colosseum symbolized the fate of Rome. As translated by Lord Byron, he declaimed, "While stands the Colosseum, Rome shall stand! When falls the Colosseum, Rome shall fall! And when Rome falls—the world!"

In the Middle Ages, when the city was divided into warring factions headed by one or another of the powerful noble families, the Colosseum was turned into a fortress by the Frangipani, who were later driven out by the Annibaldi, from whom it was wrested by the Holy Roman Emperor Henry VII. During all these wars, the building continued to fall into ruin, and by the middle of the fourteenth century the outer arches on one side had collapsed, although Gibbon declares in his *Decline and Fall of the Roman Empire* that in the middle of the sixteenth century the whole of the exterior was still inviolate. A religious order was granted jurisdiction over part of the interior, which may have helped to protect the building, but even so the structure was considered to be a ruin, little more than a source of building materials. The stones of the Colosseum were used to construct the Palazzo Farnese, part of the Cancelleria, the buildings on the Capitol, and the façade of the Palazzo Barberini. The last made use also of brass plates torn from the Pantheon and stones from so many other ancient sites that Pasquino was moved to make his famous comment, "What the barbarians did not do, the Barberini did."

Over the centuries the more enlightened popes made efforts to protect the Colosseum from further depredations, and from time to time the arena became the site of passion plays. For six years, beginning in 1671, bullfights were staged in the arena, until the exasperated Pope Clement V banned them and blocked up the lower arcades to prevent access. A cross was erected in the arena itself to commemorate the deaths of so many Christians and martyrs, and for centuries the Colosseum languished unused in the heart of Rome, a testimony to her greatness and cruelty. William W. Story, in his book *Roba di Roma* (*Stuff about Rome*), published in 1853, recalled visiting the empty stadium and commented on how "powerful and tranquil" it seemed, with swallows wheeling overhead and flocks of doves nestling among the ruins. "The place remembers not its ancient horrors, as it sleeps in the full sunlight of an Italian day—but when the shadows of night come on, and the clouds blacken above, and the wind howls through the empty galleries and arches and the storm comes down over the Colosseum, the clash of the gladiators can still be heard, the roar of the multitudinous voices crying for blood rises on the gale, and those broken benches are thronged with a fearful audience of ghosts."

I HAPPENED TO be in Rome during January 1972, when the Colosseum became the symbol to many Romans for everything that had gone wrong in the country, whose ineffective and corrupt governments had failed to solve any of the nation's most pressing economic and social problems. At the end of a damp, unpleasant day, two young Romans named Dante Ottaviani and Sabato Panico walked into the Colosseum and began to climb the rows of empty stone seats rising above the darkened arena. They were carrying a couple of blankets, some sandwiches, and a bottle of water. When they arrived at an iron grating separating the part of the edifice open to tourists from the upper arches, they climbed on over and perched at the very top of the amphitheater. A small group of friends and relatives who had watched their progress from below now announced to all who would listen that the young men were there to stay until someone did something about them; they were protesting their inability to make an honest living.

At first no one except the police paid much attention. Less than two days after they had gone up, Panico got sick and came down. Ottaviani, however, refused to budge. Dressed in pants, a turtleneck sweater, and a windbreaker, his blanket around his shoulders, he peered down, increasingly haggard-eyed, at his indifferent city. He seemed like some great angry bird. Occasionally he held up a crudely lettered sign that said, "Murderers, you've forgotten about me." To the policemen and other authorities who tried to persuade him to descend, he declared that he intended to stay in the Colosseum and, if necessary, die there rather than come back down to the same world that he felt had treated him shabbily. His sole concern, he said, was the care and feeding of his wife and baby girl. "We're not looking for luxuries—we only want to unmuck our lives," he told one of the first reporters to interview him. "It's an old story. Always hunger, from the day I was born."

By the time Ottaviani had been up there a few days, he had become a minor celebrity, primarily because his adventure made good copy and occupied portions of the city's front pages, but also because his case and what he had to say about himself and his plight, bitingly elucidated in the language of the streets, stirred up the vast reservoir of discontent under the surface of ordinary citizens' lives. "I'm all smashed up, and I've got a cold and a cough," he said on the fifth day, after a fall. "But I'm not coming down. What for? I've got nothing, and I don't want to steal. So I'll stay up here, and before I croak I'll throw my clothes down. That way, I'll die as naked as I was born."

Ottaviani's story proved to be a simple and disturbingly familiar one. His father was a bricklayer, his mother a part-time nurse, and he and a brother and two sisters had grown up in the narrow streets of the Monti, one of the older quarters of the city. When his father became ill and could no longer work, Ottaviani began to steal. He spent three years in reformatories, and later, between the ages of eighteen and twenty-three, a total of three more years inside the medieval walls of Rome's Regina Coeli prison. After the birth of a daughter in 1969, he told the press, he quit stealing. "I didn't want her to be ashamed of her father," he said. "I didn't want anyone pointing the finger at her." With a brother-in-law, he began operating a street corner stand near the railroad station, selling transistor radios, clocks, and cigarette lighters. But he didn't have a license, so the police harassed him constantly and confiscated his merchandise. Finally, after considerable difficulty, he acquired the necessary license, but was assigned an area that required a car to operate in successfully. Ottaviani could not afford a car, nor, as a convicted felon, could he even get a driver's license. His protests went unheeded, so he returned to his old corner, whereupon the cycle of arrests and confiscations resumed. All he wanted, he said now, from his refuge in the Colosseum, was a permit to sell his stuff where he could make a living, but, he added, "if I don't see something written, I'm not moving from here." When a city official trying to persuade him to come down promised that his situation would be resolved within a week, Ottaviani replied, "It's all a trick. I don't believe in anything anymore."

The presence of this solitary protester on one of the city's most famous monuments—especially one celebrated for spectacles involving the feeding of wretched Christians to lions—began to embarrass the authorities, delight tourists, and outrage the prostitutes, hustlers, and petty thieves who earned their own shabby livings within the shadows of the ancient arena. The prostitutes, hustlers, and thieves, unhappy in the glare of publicity and unable to operate successfully in the presence of so many policemen, firemen, and sundry officials, took to calling angrily up to Ottaviani to jump. The reporters, by this time, were having a field day. They showed up in clusters to interview Ottaviani and the relatives and friends who rooted for him down below and sent him up an occasional sandwich. On the seventh day, Nino Longobardi, one of the most eminent journalists in Rome, took to the pages of the daily *Il Messaggero* to comment. "We don't want to make a symbol of Dante Ottaviani, much less a hero," he wrote. "But a country that turns its back on a man alone can cause anguish in the hearts of men still truly free."

The anguish—for Dante Ottaviani and his people, at least—ended on the afternoon of the eighth day, when two city functionaries brought him a letter signed by a high official and guaranteeing him a license to operate his stand near the railroad station. Declaring himself satisfied, and complaining that his bones were aching, Ottaviani came down, and was whisked off to a hospital to recover. Within two days he disappeared from the news, but his protest was not forgotten. In the weeks afterward, a couple of hundred equally desperate people, singly and in groups, scaled other famous heights—in one case the Dome of St. Peter's itself—to roost in public and demand, almost always unsuccessfully, the happy ending granted Ottaviani. It was as if his gesture and his words spoke for the Italy that no longer counted—the people unallied with any powerful interest group, who were struggling to make themselves and their needs heard. In a story hailing the happy ending of Dante Ottaviani's ordeal, Longobardi concluded, "Meanwhile, the empty sockets of the Colosseum stare unblinkingly at us. For too long, those old stones have stood there, and they know us—ah, how they know us."

Fourteen

R OME IS A city of the illustrious and the infamous dead. There are times, when I walk about
the *centro,* that I feel the weight of all those departed
souls much as if in some way they all had played a real
part in my own life. It is impossible to go anywhere in
the city without becoming involved in its past. The
very stones you stand on are the ones over which
emperors, kings, popes, nobles, artists, soldiers, humble
folk, and history's great rascals and victims all passed in
an endless procession dating back over twenty-five
centuries to the city's founding, which began, after
all, with a murder. When Romulus struck down his
brother, Remus, to become Rome's first king, he
established a precedent for everything that followed
during the tumultuous rise and fall of an empire, the
bloody internecine struggles of the Middle Ages, even
the years of Fascism. To enjoy the city, to live in

Rome as a Roman, you have to make a separate peace with its bloody past, memorialized by some of its greatest buildings and the work of some of the country's greatest artists.

The Castel Sant'Angelo, on the banks of the Tiber, connected to the Vatican by a fortified corridor that provided various besieged popes with quick access to the safety of the castle's fortifications, began as a tomb. It was built in A.D. 135 by the Emperor Hadrian as a mausoleum for himself and his successors. Over the centuries it was converted not only into a fortress, but into a prison and place of execution. Among the many who perished here were Pope John X, suffocated; Pope Benedict VI, strangled and hurled into the Tiber; the Patriarch of Alexandria, Giovanni Vitelleschi, stabbed to death; Stefano Porcari, hanged from the battlements for having plotted against Pope Nicholas V. The Borgias used the castle to execute many of their enemies, and dozens of other citizens perished within its walls. Beatrice Cenci and members of her family were imprisoned, tortured, and tried here, as was Giordano Bruno. Giacinto Centini, accused of having used magic arts to murder Pope Urban VIII, was decapitated. Benvenuto Cellini spent time in the castle's dungeons, where many others, famous and not so famous, were locked up. Cellini actually managed to escape, but was recaptured and put into one of the most dismal of the building's prison cells, from which no one could have possibly gotten out.

I've always loved the Castel Sant'Angelo, but not because of its dark history. It's among the most cheerful of Rome's monuments, as if, in its current phase as a major tourist attraction, its intent were to undo its horrific reputation as a place of confinement, torture, and death by offering the visitor access to a series of splendid papal apartments, airy rooms, and terraces with spectacular views over the whole city. The papal quarters of Pope Paul III (1534–1549) are a case in point. They are decorated by frescoes depicting scenes from the Bible and from the life of Alexander the Great. In the so-called Camera del Perseo is a frieze showing scenes from the myth of Perseus, while the adjoining bedroom, called the Camera di Amore e Psyche, contains paintings by Mantegna, Lorenzo Lotto, and Carlo Crivelli. There is also a library, beyond which two smaller rooms are decorated with period furnishings, as well as with pictures by Dosso Dossi, Poussin, and others. Also adjacent to the library is a large circular room that was used by the popes to store their secret archives and treasure. From there a stairway leads up to the great open rooftop terrace shielded by battlements and guarded by a huge Baroque statue of the Archangel Michael sheathing his sword.

According to legend, the statue of the angel recalls a vision Pope Gregory the Great had while walking

back toward St. Peter's at the head of a religious procession he had organized to put an end to a plague
that had been decimating the city. The pope saw the
angel slowly sheathing his sword, an action that signi-
fied the end of the pestilence. The original statue was
made of wood, but was replaced by a second one, of
marble, which crumbled to pieces. The third version,
also of marble but with bronze wings, was struck by
lightning. The fourth one was melted down to make
cannonballs during the sack of Rome in 1527. The
fifth one, also of marble with bronze wings, was
replaced by the current one, made entirely of bronze.
It was already in place in 1799, when Napoleon's
army captured the city and painted the statue red,
white, and blue, stuck a beret on its head, and bap-
tized it "the Genius of France, liberator of Rome."

It was during the sack of Rome in 1527 that Pope
Clement VII, holed up safely behind the castle's thick
walls, allowed his beard to grow as a sign of distress
over the disaster overwhelming his city. Rome's cynics, however, claimed it was because he wanted to dis-
guise himself in case he was forced to flee. For the
next hundred years, until the accession to the papal
throne of Paul V (1605–1621), all the pontiffs grew
beards. The theory is they all wanted to be unrecog-
nizable just in case, a not implausible theory, given the
attitude of many Romans to their rulers. One of the
rooms in the castle contains the marble head of Pope

Paul IV erected in the Campidoglio during the closing months of his pontificate. When he died, a rioting mob smashed the statue and the head was thrown into the Tiber, from which it was later salvaged. So unpopular was this cruel pontiff that two days before his death his own canon in St. Peter's destroyed the bronze bust of Paul mounted in the sacristy.

My first visit to the rooftop terrace of the Castel Sant'Angelo came by proxy, when I first attended in Rome a performance of Giacomo Puccini's great romantic opera *La Tosca*. It was from those very battlements in the shadow of the archangel that Floria Tosca, whose lover, Mario Cavaradossi, had just been shot by a firing squad, hurled herself to her death, crying defiantly that she would confront her lover's murderer, the evil Baron Scarpia, *"davanti a Dio"* (before God)! What a moment, what a cry of defiance and revenge! Since then I've been a frequent visitor to that rooftop terrace, both in person and as a member of an audience, and I've seen at least two dozen Floria Toscas hurl themselves off the battlements. Sometimes they don't make it to the bottom. Some years ago in New York, a portly soprano threw herself off the roof, landed on the mattress springs placed to receive her, and bounced back into view. It's been hard ever since for me to take the Castel Sant'Angelo's dark and bloody history too seriously.

Fifteen

N O ONE HAS sung the glories of Rome more insistently than the celebrated movie director Federico Fellini. An adoptive Roman born in the sea-coast town of Rimini, Fellini became during his life-time so identified with the city of his choice that in nearly all of his movies, from his earliest efforts to *La Dolce Vita, Roma,* and *E la Nave Va (And the Ship Sails On)*, he seems to be exploring what it means to be a Roman. "What is Rome?" he once asked himself in a magazine interview. "And I know, more or less. I think of a big, ruddy face that resembles Sordi's, Fab-rizi's, Magnani's, its expression weighted and preoccu-pied by gastrosexual exigencies. I think of a muddy brown terrain; of an ample, broken sky, like the back-drop of an opera, a sky painted in violets, blacks, sil-ver—funereal colors. But, all in all, it's a comforting face." In many of Fellini's movies, the characters who swarm across the screen—priests, whores, officials, policemen, night owls, and street people—have a slightly ruined, corrupted look about them, an air of something noble and once beautiful allowed to decay almost beyond hope of redemption.

But Fellini's people are incredibly alive. They shout and cry and, above all, talk incessantly. They are passionately and totally involved in themselves, as unthinkingly committed as Falstaff to the small pleasures of the moment. One of my Roman friends said to me some years ago that Rome was clearly a city of cynics and people indifferent to the possibility of catastrophe. "We've survived two thousand years of foreign invasions, pillage, disasters of all sorts," he said over a sweet Vermouth at Harry's Bar on the Via Veneto. "But I doubt we can survive ten more years like the last ten. Our lives here are getting worse—even the way we see ourselves."

Nonsense, I thought. The Romans don't see themselves at all; they simply *are*. My friend, a talent agent, had been working for and with Americans for several years. Clearly he had been far more deeply corrupted than any of Fellini's people or the ones I moved among every day I spent in the city.

Romans are always predicting the worst, but then managing to overcome and survive whatever history throws their way. At the start of the twenty-sixth Holy Year, officially celebrated on Christmas Eve, 1999, during the course of the midnight Mass, the press predicted the worst possible scenario, a city about to be overrun by hordes of visitors who would make it even more ungovernable than it already was. Part of the Holy Year ceremony was the opening of the holy doors of Rome's four major basilicas—St. Peter's, San Giovanni in Laterano, Santa Maria Maggiore, and San Paolo—to admit the first of the estimated fifteen million pilgrims expected to seek indulgences. It was predicted that well over twenty-five million persons, between other Italians and visitors, would spend at least one day in the city, and what preoccupied everyone was what effect the weight of so many extra bodies would have on the city's already overloaded public facilities. Rome's ancient and primitive sewage system, for instance, has already polluted not only the Tiber but most of the nearby beaches at Ostia and Fregene, and the public transportation system, consisting mainly of buses, trolleys, and taxis, is still inadequate. "I wish the Holy Year could have been put to a vote, like the divorce law," an anticlerical Roman friend of mine in the movie business told me, "but everyone knows you can't put the presence of the Vatican to a vote, or we'd have moved it permanently to some more hospitable place, like Avignon, centuries ago."

Pessimism comes naturally to most Romans, undoubtedly because throughout the city's long history so many catastrophes have occurred. "It's always better to be prepared for the worst," my friend also observed. "That way we can never be astonished by the tricks life has prepared for us." His attitude is typically Roman, and I have learned over the years to discount it. The Romans are also famous for pretending to a total indifference toward events, fortunate or otherwise. *Menefreghismo,* which can be roughly translated as "I-don't-give-a-damnism," is a Roman specialty. The story goes that when an Italian ocean liner, the *Andrea Doria,* was struck by a Swedish ship in 1956 and began to sink, members of the crew were dispatched to warn any passengers who might still be in their cabins. A sailor who banged on the closed door of a Roman businessman's quarters was answered by a grumpy voice asking what was the matter. "Sir, the ship is sinking!" the sailor called out. "Who gives a damn," the Roman replied. "It's not mine!"

Rome is also a city in which the great Italian technique of *arrangiarsi,* which means, roughly, "getting by," has been practiced for so long that it has become an art form. This was confirmed during the recent Holy Year, when the Romans managed not to be in the least inconvenienced by the swarms of pilgrims and tourists in their streets and churches. Much was made of the fact that the visitors spent money, although there were complaints that most of the pilgrims, like the hordes of younger tourists who arrived with knapsacks on their backs in charter flights, buses, and on foot, were not the free spenders of former years. What mattered most was that the city that has proclaimed itself eternal did not crumble away over-night, destroyed by the economic vicissitudes of mod-ern times. It flourished. Everybody made money, and the Romans managed to avoid the worst of the crowding by absenting themselves during the hotter months, when the hotels, pensions, and tourist sites were most crowded.

With much of the city freed from the automobile, walking has become a rediscovered pleasure. During the hot weather, with the Romans invisible for four hours at midday behind the closed shutters and doors of their stone buildings, or streaming out of the city on weekends and holidays toward the nearby beaches, Rome itself begins to resemble more and more the huge, empty, open-air museum that many foreign tourists imagine it to be. The impression is not entirely illusory. Quite apart from the hundreds of churches, museums, and galleries open to visitors, and the famous monuments and forums, every street and piazza in the *centro storico* has become more visible, more accessible not only to the guided tours, with their swarms of confused and panting sightseers, but also to casual strollers with a desire simply to walk at random through the cornucopia of wonders that is the ancient city. The obelisks, ancient arches, famous statues, churches, and palazzi that had temporarily disappeared behind scaffolding and protective screens have reemerged, cleaned up and restored to delight the eye. A campaign, so far only partly successful, is being waged against an explosion of graffiti that defaces the walls of public buildings, and some attention is being paid to cleaning up the mounds of trash that used to be allowed to gather in the fountains and around the most celebrated of the city's treasures; the Fontana di Trevi, for instance, had become a sea of floating debris, and the delicately fluted marble columns of the Temple of the Vestal Virgins had been surrounded by soft-drink cans, bottles, papers, and even sacks of garbage.

Rome's great squares have been defended from the human pollution that for decades had converted the city into what one of its previous mayors described as the capital of a Levantine civilization. For years it was impossible much of the time to enjoy such sights as the Piazza Navona, the Pantheon, the Spanish Steps, and the Colosseum itself because of the swarms of souvenir salesmen, pushcart peddlers, and hustlers of all sorts who made of these arenas bazaars that also attracted political agitators, gangs of restless youths, and *scippatori* and other petty criminals. Not all these elements have been banished, but it has become possible again to stroll through the Piazza Navona, for instance, and enjoy the spectacle of Bernini's fountains, cleaned up at last, without having to thread one's way through crowds of questionable hangers-on.

Rome in the summer has become a festival, with outdoor concerts put on in such famous sites as the Campidoglio; theater, dance, art, and cinema, much of it free, in the streets and piazzas of the *centro*. The Romans themselves have become not only wary observers but participants in these now annual celebrations of their city's longevity. An old friend of mine, an Englishwoman who has lived in old Rome for many years, once summed up what I've always felt about the city and what keeps me coming back to it year after year. "It's not only the physical beauty of the place," she said. "It's the smell of it, the aura of great history in the stones of every street and every building. To be in Rome is to be in touch with everything in life that really matters."

Sixteen

THE WOMEN—MY grandmother, my mother, her two sisters—who took care of me and nurtured me through the years of my Roman childhood are gone now. For so many years, every time I came back to Rome, at least one or another of them would be there to greet me. They remained for decades my main points of reference to my Italian background and my years first as a little Roman schoolboy, then as a music student, later as a journalist and writer. I flourished under their tutelage and care, learning from them more about life and history and behavior than from any of the many schools I attended. My grandmother, whom I called Mammina (Little Mother) Ester, I considered the noblest Roman of them all. A fierce democrat who despised tyrants, bigots, cowards, compromising politicians, and meddling clergy, she set an example of incorruptibility that inspired me.

My Aunt Lea, a difficult, demanding personality, nevertheless had a weakness for me, because she had loved my father and I reminded her of him. She was an expert on art and taught me how to look at a painting or a sculpture, inculcated in me a curiosity to know more about the background and history of an object. For years she worked for the Frick Museum in New York, cataloguing and researching art works all over the country. Outraged by my early indifference to these timeless treasures, she had let me know in drastic terms what she thought, and sent me rushing off to museums and churches to make up for lost time. After that, she kept a wary eye on me and frequently asked me whether I had taken the time to see this or that masterpiece in whatever section of the country my travels happened to bring me to. She was a brilliant talker, with an enormous store of knowledge at her fingertips and a dangerous gift for sniffing out weaknesses in people's arguments and characters. She didn't suffer fools gladly, and was unsparing in her comments and assessments. She made her husband's life a living hell. He was my beloved Uncle Akos, a Hungarian noble, a deeply civilized man who had earned a comfortable living as a screenwriter and movie producer for many years, but who in Lea's eyes had never lived up to her expectations of him. She berated him for his weaknesses, his failings, and eventually forced him to flee from her. Her rages and inner torments brought her to the brink of madness, from which she was rescued by electroshock treatment and months of therapy, but she and Akos never reconciled. They each spent their last years living alone, Lea dying in a nursing home, Akos in their daughter Flavia's apartment. He slipped out of life in his sleep, leaving as gently as he had lived. Lea's legacy to me was a memory of her coruscating wit, her immense knowledge of the arts, her prodding, penetrating intelligence.

My Aunt Franca was the older sister I never had. All during my childhood in Rome and on the island of Capri, where my mother, my grandmother, and I lived for two years in the early 1930s, she whisked me off on excursions that inevitably became adventures. We'd romp together in the Villa Borghese, tour the zoo, visit churches and museums, spend hours in the fascinating recesses of the Castel Sant'Angelo or some other great monument, go boating around Capri, picnic on beaches, and steal grapes from a peasant's vineyard, escaping with the angry owner in full pursuit. I never knew what Franca would come up with next, only that it would be new, exciting, devoted to the pleasures of discovery. Franca's weakness was men. Not conventionally beautiful, she had a slim, lovely figure, with stunning legs, was graceful, musical, cheerful, and enormously attractive to the male. As usual, Lea had the final say about her. "She needs the smell of a man around her," she observed one day, during the middle of a crisis brought on by Franca's passionate involvement with a painter named Emmanuele Cavalli, for whom she had left her husband, a Swiss businessman. She went to live with Cavalli and his wife in Florence, an arrangement that eventually caused a breakdown. My grandmother went north to rescue her and her son, and bring them both back to Rome. She continued to frequent the company of artists, most of whom I met and several of whom became friends of mine after my return to Rome in 1947. Later she became involved with and married a film editor, whose two teenaged sons she helped to raise. In the end their marriage failed because of his alcoholism and intemperate behavior. By that time she, too, had gone to work in the movie business. For eight years she and Lea did not speak, but in the end the sisters made peace, and it was Franca who went to see Lea faithfully several times a week toward the end of Lea's life. Franca herself died abruptly, unexpectedly, seated over a dinner tray in front of her television set in her small apartment in the *centro storico*.

My mother, the oldest of the three Danesi sisters, outlived them. She had had the most brilliant career of the three of them, first as an actress and singer, then as a daily shortwave broadcaster to Italy for NBC in New York. When the Second World War broke out and the Office of War Information took over the program, my mother became, in effect, the voice of

America to Italy during the hostilities. Soon after the liberation of Rome, she was sent to Italy, where she helped establish a free Italian press, while rooting out Fascists from the world of arts and letters. Back in New York, she became the American representative for Mondadori, one of Italy's major publishers of books and magazines, and bought the works of important writers for publication in Italy. When Mondadori installed a new regime my mother didn't like, she took over the New York office of Rizzoli, Mondadori's great rival. During her last years, into her nineties, she represented a smaller Italian publishing house, Sperling and Kupfer, continuing her work of bringing American authors to the attention of the Italian reading public. She died at ninety-two in my house in San Diego, California, the last member of my immediate Roman family. Now, whenever I go back to Rome, the streets seem emptier and haunted by the ghosts of these four Roman women who meant so much to me.

There is a Danesi family tomb in the cemetery of the Verano, not far from the Church of San Lorenzo. It is marked by a small monument surrounded by four marble columns and bearing the names of two earlier Danesi sisters who died in the 1800s. From time to time the tomb, like all the others in the Verano, has to be opened. Workmen go inside to remove the remains of cadavers, which have become little more than bones and rags, from their coffins and place them in much smaller zinc containers that are then labeled and stacked in ranks along the walls. The larger coffins are removed, thus creating space for the newer arrivals. It's the only way these burying grounds can continue to accommodate the generations of the dead over the hundreds of years the Verano has functioned as Rome's main cemetery. The area once belonged to a rich Roman matron named Veranus, who founded the cemetery to inter there the corpses of Christian martyrs, including San Lorenzo himself. The Danesi tomb, watched over and tended now by my cousin Flavia, Lea's daughter, includes the remains of my grandmother and my two aunts, all still in their original coffins but scheduled eventually to be tucked away into their zinc boxes among the ranks of the long departed. Each time a tomb is opened and any changes are made, approval has to be secured from the Department of Antiquities and Fine Arts, which guards the older sections of the cemetery as it would any other of Rome's historic areas. The Verano, with its ancient tombs, has become another of the city's tourist sights, and visitors, in small groups of fewer than a dozen people, can be observed daily strolling past the rows of monuments and tombstones, guidebooks in hand.

My mother chose not to be interred in the Verano. She wanted to have her ashes, along with those of her dearest friend and lover, the journalist Janet Flanner of

The New Yorker, scattered into the waters of the Atlantic at Cherry Grove, on Fire Island, New York, where she had spent many happy summers. I honored her wishes. But I think that some portion of her still lingers in the streets of Rome, and I feel her presence in the city as vividly as I do those of her sisters and my beloved Mammina Ester. Rome is so many things, but most of all, perhaps, a city of ghosts, of memories, of visions, of time remembered and faithfully honored.

About the Author

WILLIAM MURRAY is the author of more than twenty books, including *Italy: The Fatal Gift* and *The Last Italian*. He was a staff writer for *The New Yorker* and has contributed to the *New York Times* magazine, *The Nation, Playboy,* and *Esquire.* He lives in Del Mar, California.

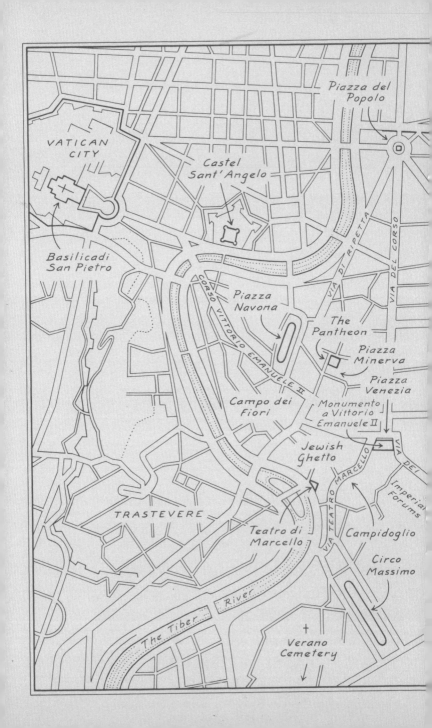